MW00889216

Japan Travel Guide

Culture, food, experiences, sights, buildings, museums, shrines, temples, parks, areas and more in Tokyo, Kyoto, Yokohama, Osaka, Nagoya, Sapporo, Kobe and Mt. Fuji

Table of Contents

Introduction

Japan is truly timeless, a place where ancient traditions are fused with modern life as if it were the most natural thing in the world.

Traditional Culture

On the surface, Japan appears exceedingly modern, but travelling around it offers numerous opportunities to connect with the country's traditional culture. Spend the night in a ryokan (traditional Japanese inn), sleeping on futons and tatami mats, and padding through well-worn wooden halls to the bathhouse (or go one step further and sleep in an old farmhouse). Chant with monks or learn how to whisk bitter matcha (powdered green tea) into a froth. From the splendor of a Kyoto geisha dance to the spare beauty of a Zen rock garden, Japan has the power to enthrall even the most jaded traveler.

Food

Wherever you are in Japan, it seems, you're never more than 500m from a great meal. Restaurants often specialize in just one dish – perhaps having spent generations perfecting it – and pay close attention to every stage, from sourcing the freshest, local ingredients to assembling the dish attractively. Moreover, you don't have to travel far to discover that

Japanese cuisine is deeply varied. The hearty hotpots of the mountains are, for example, dramatically different from the delicate sushi for which the coast is famous. It's also intensely seasonal, meaning you can visit again at a different time of year and experience totally new tastes.

Outdoors

Japan is a long and slender, highly volcanic archipelago. It's over two-thirds mountains, with bubbling hot springs at every turn. In the warmer months there is excellent hiking, through cedar groves and fields of wildflowers, up to soaring peaks and ancient shrines (the latter founded by wandering ascetics). In the winter, all this is covered with snow and the skiing is world class. (And if you've never paired hiking or skiing with soaking in onsen, you don't know what you've been missing.) Meanwhile in the southern reaches, there are tropical beaches for sunning, snorkeling, diving and surfing.

Dynamic Cities

The neon-lit streetscapes of Japan's cities look like sci-fi film sets, even though many of them are decades old. Meanwhile, cities such as Tokyo and Osaka have been adding new architectural wonders that redefine what buildings – and cities – should look like. There's an indelible buzz to these urban centers, with their vibrant street life, 24-hour drinking and dining scenes, and creative hubs that turn out fashion and pop culture trends consumed the world over. Travel is always smooth and efficient, whether you're using the subway to get around or the shinkansen (bullet trains) to go from one city to the next.

First things you need to know about Japan

If you have been dreaming of traveling to Japan and want to start planning your vacation, this travel guide is packed with all the tips and information that you'll need to know before your trip to the "land of the rising sun".

From foods to try in Japan, to how much money to budget, to what travel gear to pack, I 're covering everything. And I mean everything! I 're even answering your embarrassing questions like, "What are the toilets like in Japan?"

I am sharing exactly how much it costs to travel to Japan, and I am throwing in some money-saving budget tips! This is the ultimate resources with everything you need to know before visiting Japan for the first time.

Transportation in Japan is incredibly efficient and comfortable, but it ain't cheap! To save the most money, purchase a 7-day JR Pass and you won't regret it. If you plan to visit more than 1 region, the pass quickly pays for itself – just a roundtrip from Kyoto to Tokyo is enough to make up the steep Price. (Plus, you get to ride the famous Japanese bullet trains which is a bucket list experience in itself!)

Why should Japan be on your travel bucket list?

Japan is a surprising combination of peace and chaos, old and new and has just the right amount of quirkiness to make it an addicting place to visit that will have you coming back for more!

Best times of year to visit Japan

If you're considering a trip to Japan, you're probably wondering what time of year is best to visit. The wonderful thing is every season is a great time to visit Japan, and you will have a completely unique experience. I 'll lay out what to expect in each season, as well as the pros and cons of visiting during these times.

Note: The weather is based on averages, though it can vary a lot throughout the country.

Japan in the Spring (March - May)

Cherry blossoms in bloom; lots of festivals

Pleasant temperatures and not much rain

Lots of crowds for cherry blossoms

Japan in the Summer (June - August)

Hot and humid weather

3-4-week rainy period (usually mid-June through mid-July)

Festivals and fireworks starting in July

Mount Fuji is opened for climbing in July

Good time for beach holidays in places like Okinawa

Japan in the Fall (September - November)

Colorful leaves make the landscape spectacular (October is the best month for leaves)

Temperatures are comfortable

Lots of festivals, concerts, sports tournaments and exhibitions during this time

Less crowds

Japan in the Winter (December - February)

Less crowds

Skiing in Japan is said to be some of the best in the world!

Ideal temperature for soaking in outdoor onsens

Small towns look magical covered in snow

Before you book a trip to Japan in the spring, know this...

Spring is considered by many as a great time to visit Japan for its comfortable temperatures, cherry blossoms and little chance of rain.

One thing you should be aware of is the so-called "Golden Week" which falls in the springtime and is made up of 4 national holidays which fall into a 7-day span. This means many Japanese people will also be traveling around the country and accommodation and tours are often booked far in advance.

Golden Week in Japan Dates

2018: April 28 - May 6

2019: April 27 - May 12 (Holidays are more spread out)

Fun Facts about Japan

These facts will be good conversation starters with other travelers or even locals! So break that ice and let them in on some fun facts about Japan!

Japan has an average of 1,500 earthquakes each year!

6,852 islands make up the country of Japan.

There are more than 200 volcanoes in Japan.

Vending machines are super popular in Japan -- there are more than 5.5 million of them around the country and they dispense everything from snacks to fresh eggs to toilet paper. (And some weirder stuff that a quick Google search that reveal to you.)

The literacy rate in Japan is nearly 100%.

The first geishas were men. (The word "geisha" means person of the arts.)

Do I need a Tourist Visa to visit Japan?

There are 66 countries in total where their citizens do not require a visa to enter Japan, but the time you can stay depends on which country you're from.

Citizens from many countries (including the U.S.A., the U.K., Canada, and Australia) get a visa exemption (a.k.a. FREE) 90-day tourist visa, provided they will not be working in Japan.

Other countries get a temporary tourist visa for a period of 15 days or less.

To find out the specifics for your country, check out the Japan National Tourism Organization, which explains the requirements for each country.

How safe is Japan?

Japan is overall very safe and crime is low. I once met a girl who was an English teacher in Tokyo, and she said she left her wallet in a train station. It sat there, untouched, and the next day when she retraced her steps it was in the same (heavily trafficked) place she had left it.

But even though theft isn't common in Japanese culture, that doesn't mean it can't happen to you. As with any place in the world, always be aware of your surroundings and use common sense. And I always recommend getting travel insurance to make sure you're covered in case anything gets stolen or you run into other emergencies.

Do I need a power converter in Japan?

In Japan the standard voltage is 100 V and the power sockets are type A and B. The socket is the same used in North America, but the voltage is lower, so yes you will need a power converter for electronics that don't already have a converter.

What are the bathrooms like in Japan?

This might be an embarrassing question to ask out loud, but I promise you aren't the only one thinking it. If it's your first time visiting Japan, you likely have no idea what to expect when it comes to bathrooms.

The good news is, many bathrooms around the country are very nice and quite... luxurious. In nicer restrooms, you'll find toilets equipped with a built-in bidet to spray your bum. And some toilets even have buttons that will play music or rainforest sounds to cover up, well, you know...

Be warned though that in some train stations or in more rural parts of the country, you may find squat toilets similar to ones you'd find in many places around Asia.

How to get cell phone service in Japan

First, I will say that it is not necessary to get a SIM card during your travels in Japan. WiFi is common, and you'll find it in most hotels or hostels, as well as in several coffee shops and restaurants around the country.

While in WiFi, you can easily talk with friends and family back at home through apps like Skype and Facebook Messenger, and you can connect with locals using WhatsApp.

That said, if you really want to get cell service with a data plan so you always have Internet access, it is possible to buy a Japanese SIM card. (You have to make sure your phone is unlocked and has the capability to accept a foreign SIM card -- I found out the hard way!)

Helpful free apps for travel in Japan

Google Navigation: Can give you the best routes for the metro and trains and even has live updates on delays.

Hyperdia: The go-to train scheduling app/website in Japan. Plug in a route and it will tell you the times throughout the day and the Prices, including each seating class.

Google Translate: This is a go-to app for us while traveling in Asia because you can take a photograph of the characters on a menu or label and it will translate for you. Be warned that some things don't quite translate into English all that well...

GuruNavi Restaurant Guide: I 've been told this is the app you should use to find restaurants over TripAdvisor because the latter has more reviews from foreigners than locals. GuruNavi is easy to use and will point you in the direction of hole-in-the-wall places where locals eat instead of the typical tourist haunts.

Japan Travel Guide With Me: This app has all sorts of useful information for your travels in Japan, and the best part is it can be used offline.

What is the currency in Japan?

In Japan, the currency is yen (¥). The current exchange rate (Jan 2018) is as follows:

USD: $1 = ¥110

British Pound: £1 = ¥153

Euro: €1 = ¥135

CAD: $1 = ¥88

Australian Dollar: $1 = ¥88

Are credit cards accepted in Japan?

Yes, but hold up... Major credit cards will typically be accepted at big hotel chains, nice restaurants or shops in large cities, but you'll want to have cash on hand to use in small restaurants, markets or in more rural towns. There are still many places where credit cards are not accepted, so it is a good idea not to rely on your plastic alone.

Should I get money from my bank before my trip to Japan?

This is a question I get all the time. The answer really comes down to your personal preference, but I never get money out in advance anymore.

Whenever I enter a new country, I walk right past the "Currency Exchange" counters (they are a huge rip off most of the time!) and I go to an ATM to withdraw cash. You will get the best exchange rate possible at an ATM.

If the thought of showing up in a new country without cash on hand makes your hands sweaty, then by all means ignore this advice and grab some yen from your home bank before you leave.

But I will say that airports always have ATMS, and they are easy to find in train stations as well as in 7-Eleven's and Family Marts in most big Japanese cities. Before heading to a rural town though, be sure to take out cash just in case you can't find an ATM.

Credit card travel tips

Be sure to alert your bank ahead of time that you will be traveling so they know your transactions aren't fraud.

Also, it's a good idea to carry more than one card in case you have an issue with one of them. And carry them in two different locations -- for example, one in your wallet and another in your backpack so in save one gets lost or stolen, you still have access to the other.

How much does Japan cost?

I know it can be helpful to see an idea of how much certain things cost to give you an idea of how much you'll be paying. These are all average Prices in Tokyo, and this is only meant to give you a baseline. You can find these items cheaper or you can pay much more. Also, Prices will vary around the country.

Average costs in Tokyo

Budget: ¥3,000 for a dorm bed (around $27 USD)

Mid-range: ¥5,000 - 10,000 for a private room in a guesthouse or cheap hotel ($45 - $90 USD)

High-end: ¥10,000 - 30,000 for a Western style hotel or more luxurious ryokan ($90 - $270 USD)

Bowl of ramen: ¥800 at a restaurant ($7 USD), ¥300 at a convenience store ($2.75 USD)

Train from Kyoto to Tokyo: ¥13,080 one-way ($120 USD) Now you see why everyone gets the Japan Rail pass.

Subway pass for the day: ¥700 per person ($6.40 USD)

Coffee: ¥300 ($2.75 USD)

How much to budget for one week in Japan

I'll be straight to the point: Japan is not cheap. Contrary to many other destinations in Asia, like Thailand or the Philippines, Japan is not an ideal location for budget travelers. That said, it is unlike any country in the world and totally worth visiting.

I 'll break down about how much money you should plan to budget for a trip in Japan based on your travel style.

*Note: These are estimations for one person and do not include flights.

Budget Traveler: $450 USD per week

You'll stay in hostel dorm beds, grab breakfast from one of the many 7-Eleven's or Family Marts, and will do as many free activities as possible.

Mid-Range Traveler: $850 USD per week

You'll be staying in comfortable, though not fancy, hotels or Airbnbs. You'll want to try lots of Japanese food -- both budget meals and a couple nicer ones too. You will use public transportation to get around and you want to see as much as possible, but you're willing to make some sacrifices to save money.

High-end Traveler: $2,000 USD per week

Budget isn't too much of a concern for you. This isn't necessarily luxury travel, but you are willing to pay more money for convenience and comfort; and splurging on unique, once-in-a-lifetime experiences is not a problem for you.

Money-saving tips in Japan

While it's not a cheap country to visit, there are certainly ways you can save money while traveling in Japan.

Buy a Japan Rail Pass if you plan to venture outside of Tokyo.

Get your breakfasts and snacks at 7-Eleven or Family Mart (they are everywhere around the country!). While you might never consider eating at a convenience store in your home country, the fresh food options are surprisingly good at these stores in Japan. I'm not joking. You'll see many locals doing the same.

Have your biggest meal midday and take advantage of "lunch sets" which often consist of a large meal (sometimes with a dessert) and are typically between $5-7 USD.

Conveyor belt sushi is a good way to try all the types of sushi your little heart (and stomach!) desire without a huge Price tag. Plus, it's a fun experience in itself!

Use an app to record your spending and see how well you're staying on top of your budget! I find it's much easier to overspend when you don't know how much it's all adding up to. I love Trail Wallet for recording expenses.

How to get around Japan

One of the most expensive parts about travel in Japan is the transportation. That said, you get what you pay for. The trains and metros in Japan are some of the cleanest and most efficient in the world.

The best way to save money on trains is to buy the Japan Rail Pass. I know, I know, it is a big Price to pay up front, but I 've done all the calculations, and simply put: if you plan to visit both Tokyo and Kyoto, buying the pass will save you money.

Also, in major cities, there are sometimes "package deals" on transportation. In Tokyo, I found the 24-hour metro pass to be well worth the Price, and in Kyoto, the all-day bus pass was a money-saving purchase.

What are the trains like in Japan?

Overall, the trains are clean, comfortable and efficient. The rail system covers almost the entire country, making it a wonderful way to get around.

Language in Japan & Useful Japanese Words

The language in Japan is, quite obviously, Japanese. But many people in big cities, like Tokyo, Kyoto and Osaka also speak English.

Signs are written in Japanese characters, and in the cities most have their Roman counterparts.

Japanese phrases and words to learn

When traveling, I always try to learn a couple important phrases. It shows locals you are trying to learn about their country and it can be fun too!

These phrases are ones I have found to be the most useful in any location I visit:

Hello: Kon'nichiwa

Thank you: Arigato

Thank you very much: Domo Arigato

Beer, please: Biru kudasai

Cheers! Kanpai

Bathroom: Basurumu

How much? Ikura

Delicious: Oishi

Beautiful: Kireina

Manners and customs in Japan

When traveling in a country other than your own, it is always a good idea to do a little research on what is polite so that you don't accidentally offend people like this.

Here are couple manners to keep in mind when traveling to Japan:

- Eating while you walk is considered sloppy. Instead, find a place to sit and enjoy your snack.
- Pointing is considered rude. Instead, use an open hand to make gestures.
- Blowing your nose in public can be considered rude. Japanese people often go into the bathroom to blow a stuffy nose.
- On a crowded subway or train, it is polite to take off your backpack and hold it in your hands.
- Slurping noodles not only cools them down as you eat, but it indicates that the meal is delicious. So slurp away, it's the polite thing to do!
- Taking off your shoes is common courtesy before entering many places. If the floor is raised at the doorway, it is an indicator that you should remove your shoes.

What is the tipping culture in Japan?

Should I tip at restaurants in Japan? This is a question I always ask ourselves once I reach a new country, and it is never fun being caught off guard, unsure of what to do.

In Japan, tips are not expected, and can even be considered rude. And even if the server is not offended, they will likely be confused.

What is the religion in Japan?

Buddhism and Shinto are the main religions in Japan, though they don't play a huge role in the lives of many Japanese people today.

All throughout the country, you can visit temples and shrines to get a better understanding of the religions and culture. You can even do a temple stay in order to really delve in and learn about Buddhism.

Foods to try in Japan

Japanese cuisine stretches far beyond the sushi rolls I 've come to associate with this country. (Though of course you must try sushi from the source while you're in Japan!)

Unagi (freshwater eel)

If this word brings to mind images of Ross on Friends with fingers to his temple, then I will get along well. And since I 're friends now, I'm going to tell you that unagi is life-changing. Not the "state of total awareness" life-changing that Ross speaks of, but in the "I never thought eel could taste so good" way. I've always been slightly creeped out by eels, and the prospect of eating one wasn't too appetizing. But I'm so glad I did. And not just in a sushi roll - but on its own. It melts in your mouth and has a uniquely delicate flavor you just have to taste for yourself.

Okonomiyaki

Okonomi meaning "what you like" and yaki meaning "grilled", this savory pancake is literally, well, "grilled how you like". The batter and toppings vary throughout the country, but if you want the traditional version, head to Osaka where the dish is said to have originated. I ordered okonomiyaki in Osaka and were rewarded with a generous portion of flower and egg batter filled with cabbage, yam, pork belly and green onions. No wonder this round, topping-heavy dish is often called "Japanese pizza".

Takoyaki

Sometimes referred to as "octopus balls", this popular Japanese snack is a lot more delicious than the name implies. These balls made of batter are stuffed with chopped octopus, then topped with flavorful sauces, pickled ginger, tempura and green onions. You'll find these crowded stands in markets by day, and on busy streets at night.

Green Tea Ice Cream

The tea in Japan is different than the loose leaf variety you may be used to. Instead of leaving them whole, the leaves are ground into a fine powder called matcha. In Japan, green tea is not just a beverage. There is green tea flavored EVERYTHING! Lip gloss, KitKat bars, and yes, ice cream. You'll find a bevy of soft serve shops all doling out the same specialty - green tea flavor. If you've never tried it before, beware that it can actually be quite bitter. Try it paired with vanilla for a sweeter experience!

Ramen

I'm not talking about those packages of dried noodles you lived off of during your college years. Picture freshly made noodles, broth with a depth of flavors, tender pork and a soft boiled egg cooked to perfection. Piled high on top is roasted vegetables, green onions and fresh ginger. Okay, gotta stop now. My mouth is watering.

The packaged square variety is a distant cousin to this culinary star, which is becoming popular around the world. But just like sushi, there aren't many better places to try it than in Japan. Tokyo has noodle shops on nearly every street, so try a few!

Tip: Most ramen shops have a vending machine of sorts, from which you will purchase a ticket. Hand the slip to one of the workers and they'll whip up your dish in front of your eyes.

Yakisoba

This mixture of fried noodles and vegetables is a common street food. For a fun meal, pick a restaurant where you can belly-up to your very own hotplate. I had meat and eggs added and cooked it ourselves before indulging in fried noodle yumminess.

Nikuman

These steamed pork buns are light, fluffy and are a perfect snack to warm you up on a cold day. Pick up a couple at one of the countless 7-elevens for a snack on the go.

Sushi

I know, I know, no surprise here. But it made the list because you just can't go to Japan and not try sushi. It would be like going to Italy and not eating pasta. Compared to other meals in Japan, sushi is not all that expensive. So order it often! Try a conveyor belt restaurant where you can pick each piece off the moving counter beside you. And if you're in Tokyo, make the journey to the famous Tjujuki Fish market where you can order the freshest fish in all of Japan. And best yet, take a sushi-making class and make your own rolls like I did!

Udon

This hot soup comes brimming with thick noodles and is both simple and satisfying. The best part? The Price tag is usually under $5 USD, making it a great lunch option for budget travelers.

Tonkatsu (pork katsu)

Truth be told, I'm really not a pork person. I'm also not really a fan of deep fried things. So there's two reasons I thought I wouldn't like tonkatsu - deep fried pork cutlet. This popular Japanese dish surprised me though. While staying in the small mountain town of Hakone, I wandered into a traditional Japanese restaurant. I ordered a chicken dish (which was delicious) and Ben ordered pork katsu. It arrived on a bed of rice, shredded cabbage and smothered in a tasty brown sauce and I found myself stealing bite after bite.

Travel in Japan with allergies

Traveling with dietary restrictions can be challenging, but it's not impossible. Here is some information on specific allergies and restrictions that can help you plan your time in Japan.

Gluten Free in Japan

Japanese cuisine doesn't appear to be heavy on wheat, so it might surprise you to learn that gluten is found in lots of Japanese dishes. Many of the staple sauces (including soy sauce and miso) have wheat in them.

Many Japanese people are unfamiliar with gluten-free eating, so it can be a bit tricky to find food that will work for you if you can't eat gluten.

Vegetarian / Vegan in Japan

Vegetarian and vegan restaurants are becoming increasingly popular in cosmopolitan parts of Japan, but it can still be very difficult to navigate menus if you don't read Japanese.

Here are some tips for vegetarians traveling in Japan:

Happy Cow is a great website that lists vegetarian/vegan restaurants all around the world!

Dashi is a fish stock base that is in many dishes, even if they don't contain meat. Be careful when ordering soups, or ask waitstaff if the dish contains dashi. Miso soup, however, is typically suitable for vegans.

Conveyor belt sushi restaurants are a good place to find vegetarian food as they often have veggie rolls, avocado rolls and cucumber rolls, as well as a variety of desserts.

Okonomiyaki is a good dish to try, as it is made to order and you can customize the ingredients to your liking.

Allergies or other Dietary Restrictions in Japan

If you have any dietary restrictions, it might be a good idea to print out these cards and carry them with you during your trip in Japan. They explain your dietary restrictions in Japanese so staff at any restaurant is sure to understand what ingredients you can and cannot eat.

Best cities to visit on your first time in Japan

Japan is a huge country, and it would be an extensive list if I went through all the notable cities to visit. But if you are visiting Japan for the first time, these cities are a good place to start as they will give you a good taste of the country's culture and are relatively easy to get to and from.

Tokyo - This huge metropolis is likely where you're flying in and out of, and it is one of the most interesting cities I 've visited anywhere in the world. From quirky experiences, to amazing foods, Tokyo is definitely worth some time on your itinerary.

Kyoto - Packed with history, important temples, gorgeous architecture and a charming atmosphere, this city is a favorite on many Japan itineraries. If you are traveling with your little ones, there are tons of things to do in Kyoto with kids.

Osaka - Another major hub to fly in and out of Japan, Osaka is worth a visit. It's full of history and food, and is a good city to have a night out with friends. And if you're wondering what to do, check out this list of things to do in Osaka.

Hakone - At the footsteps of Mt. Fuji, Hakone is a peaceful retreat from the big cities of Japan and a chance to relax in an onsen and sleep in a ryokan.

Top sights to see on your first time in Japan

Mount Fuji - The most famous mountain in Japan, you can get a glimpse of this beauty when traveling in Hakone.

Fushimi Inari Taisha Shrine - Known to tourists as the "Orange Gates", there are thousands of majestic orange gates covering a maze of paths leading up to the shrine.

Arashiyama - Located on the western edge of Kyoto, Arashiyama is an area that is filled with temples and shrines, but the main attraction is the Arashiyama Bamboo Grove.

Temples in Japan - Of course temples will be on your list of things to see in Japan. The Golden Pavilion in Kyoto is stunning with the garden setting and reflection off the pond.

Shibuya Intersection - Famously known as the "busiest intersection in the world" crossing the street here is quite an experience.

Note: I have not been to Nara Deer Park, so I can't personally attest to this popular attraction. I have heard that visitors are able to feed the deer with crackers that are for sale on site. I am typically against the feeding of wild animals, and would urge anyone visiting Nara Park to do a little research on the topic.

Unique experiences in Japan

One of the many reasons Japan is such a wonderful place to visit is there are so many unique experiences that can only be had in this country. Here are just a few of the things that are quintessentially "Japanese".

Soak in an Onsen - strip down to your birthday suit and soak in a hot tub until you get pruney. Don't worry, they are gender separated and some are even private. The best one I dipped in was in the Hakone region.

Take your picture in a Photo Booth - Pop in one these with your friends and take a few snaps. Then, edit your photos instantly, enhancing your eyes, adding blush, or slimming your cheeks. It takes the work selfie to a whole new level.

See the Nara Deer - Just a little way outside of Osaka, there is a park (and part of the city) literally flooded with cute spotted deer. They are quite tame, but please do not feed wild animals.

Jigokudani Snow Monkeys - A few miles away from Nagano, there is a park where the local macaque monkeys soak in a spring-fed hot tub and play around in the snow.

Stay at a Ryokan - Experience a traditional Japanese-style inn and stay at ryokan to enjoy in Japanese hospitality and relaxation.

Take a Japanese cooking class - Learn how to make proper sushi or traditional ramen to impress your friends at home.

Sleep in a Temple - Usually taken as retreats to refresh your body and mind or deepen understanding of religion, temple stays are a unique experience you won't forget.

Themed Cafes - From vampire cafes to butler cafes to prison-themed restaurants, there are quirky cafes for every interest. There are also animal cafes such as dog and cat cafes too.

Responsible Travel Tip: Be cautious about animal tourism. Domesticated animal cafes (like dog or cat cafes) seem to take care of their animals. But for non-domesticated animals cafes, like owl cafes, I would just be a little hesitant to visit.

Go Geisha hunting - On the old street of Kyoto, Geisha scurry from one event to the next. Try to get a glimpse of them, or better yet try to get a picture.

Theme restaurant - This was one of the craziest dinners I ever attended! Eat your dinner as robots fight right in front of you to techno music and laser lights. It's an unforgettable experience.

See the fish auction each morning - Show up around 3 a.m. (yep, that early) as the fishermen come in to port and sell their fish at the Tsukiji Fish Market. Then find a shop and have the freshest sushi you'll ever eat.

Go skiing or snowboarding - Japan boasts some of the best ski resorts and mountains in the world. If you have the chance to hit the slopes, don't hesitate.

Watch a Sumo wrestling match: There are 6 sumo matches held each year. If you're lucky enough to be there at the right time, don't miss the opportunity! Three matches are held in Tokyo (January, May and September) and one each in Osaka (March), Nagoya (July) and Fukuoka (November).

Free (or cheap) things to do in Japan

Japan is not the cheapest travel destination, but there are some free and inexpensive activities you can take advantage of to keep your wallet happy!

Free Walking Tours: You'll meet other travelers and learn stories and information that you'd never find out on your own! You can find walking tours in the bigger cities, like Kyoto Free Walking Tour, Osaka Free Walking Tour and Tokyo Free Walking Tour.

Visiting Temples: many temples are free to enter and explore

Parks: Meiji Shrine is not far away from Tokyo and it is free to enter. The Arashiyama bamboo grove in Kyoto is also free to explore on your own.

Join a meet up: There are plenty of meet up groups that you can find online. Simply Google "Meetups in _____." Here is the Meetup site for Tokyo.

Explore markets: There are thousands of markets all throughout Japan. You can't miss the Tsukiji Fish Market in Tokyo or the Nishiki Market in Kyoto. The walking street/restaurant haven in Dotonbori area in Osaka.

Festivals & cultural events in Japan

In Japan, festivals are called "matsuri" and they take place all year long. This is a list of some of the more unique festivals in Japan.

Jan 15: Nozawa Fire Festival, in Nagano, Japan

Feb 5-12: Sapporo Yuki Matsuri (Snow Festival), Sapporo, Hokkaido

Late March: Sumo Wrestling Spring Basho, Osaka

Early June: The Kaiko Kinenbi, Yokohama Port Opening Ceremony (Boat Races)

July: Shounan Hiratsuka Tanabata Matsuri (Star Festival), Hiratsuka

Late July: Tenjin Matsuri (Festival of the Gods), Osaka

October: Warai Festival (Laughing Festival), Wakayama

Japan trip ideas based on your interest

Japan is more than just Tokyo. If it's your first time traveling to the "Land of the Rising Sun", I'd definitely recommend a visit to its capital city as well as some of the other more well-known places like Kyoto and Osaka. But, if you have "been there done that", or you have a lot of time to play with, here are some ideas for a trip more suited to your interests.

Japan for families

If you're traveling to Japan with children, here are some ideas that are great for families with kids of all ages:

Nara Deer Park: See 1,200 adorable and friendly deer roaming freely around this park.

Amusement Park(s): There are many to choose from, including DisneySea Tokyo, DisneyLand Tokyo and Universal Studios (which includes the Wizarding World of Harry Potter).

Hitatchi Seaside Park: Popular with families for the millions of flowers that bloom all year round, ferries wheel, putt-putt golf and bike paths, this could be a nice day trip from Tokyo.

Koizumi Bokujo Farm - Visit a Japanese dairy farm where your family can learn about the animals and nature. You can even feed or milk the cows if you like. Oh and don't forget to get some ice cream from the farm shop before you leave.

Japan for couples

Japan can actually be an incredibly romantic place, depending on the destinations you choose.

Okinawa: If you're looking for a romantic beach getaway, this may be just what you're looking for!

Shirakawa: Tucked away in the mountains of Central Japan, this UNESCO historical village is stunning.

Kurashiki: Sometimes referred to as the "Amsterdam of Japan" for its canals and charming architecture, it's easy to see the romantic appeal of this town.

Park Hyatt Hotel in Tokyo: Have a drink at Lost in Translation hotel. It's an incredible view overlooking one of the largest cities in the world. You can pretend your Bill Murray and the other Scarlett Johannson.

Japan for nature lovers

Despite having some of the largest and busiest cities in the world, there is so much nature to be explored in Japan, especially in the mountains. There are plenty of incredible hiking trails throughout Japan, so make sure you pack your hiking boots.

Mount Fuji: The icon of Japan is open for hiking during the peak season of July and August when the mountain huts are open.

Takachiho Gorge: Walk along or even boat through the mossy green gorge in the Miyazaki region of Kyushu Island. The Tatsuzawa Fudo no Taki Waterfall ends the 1 km trail near a Buddhist temple.

Cedar Avenue in Hakone: It's a preserved section of the historic Tokaido Road, this area has over 400 Cedar trees towering over the forest floor.

Tottori Sand Dunes: Stretching over 2 km and rising up to 45 meters high, these dunes are a famous attraction with a sand sculpture museum.

Mount Tateyama: It has the highest peak of the Toyama mountains and is one of the three sacred mountains of Japan, after Mt. Fuji and Hakusan.

Japan off the beaten path

Shinjuku's Golden Gai Bar Crawl: Tucked away in a corner of Tokyo, these 6 narrow streets are home to a variety of micro bars that can only fit a handful of people, some only 3 or 4 seats. Most of these establishments have their own themes as well, so be sure to try the rocker bar and the French-themed bar.

Yamachan: What?! An all-you-can-drink premium sake bar?! And you can bring in your own food. Am I in Japanese heaven? Located near Shinjuku, you won't find many tourists in this self-service pour your own drink bar.

Tokyo Free Guide: Request the service of a free guide from this non-profit organization. They are free of charge and can take you on a tour anywhere you want to go and they are happy and informative guides.

Jidayubori Park Old Farmhouse Garden: Built in the Edo period (1800's), the series of farmhouses are maintained by an elderly couple who lived in them during the 20th century.

Haunted Tokyo Tour: Ready for a good scare? Choose between one of 6 tours that will bring you around Tokyo in search of ghosts of samurais and spooky graveyards. The guide speaks multiple languages and bring you to not-so-popular places in Tokyo.

Japan for foodies

Japanese cuisine is renowned around the world, and there's nothing quite like trying it at the source. Foodies will love Japan for its fresh ingredients and careful attention to technique.

Tsukiji Fish Market: Get the freshest sushi you will ever taste. It's better than you can ever imagine.

Cooking Class: Learn how to make your favorite Japanese dishes and then bring your skills back home to impress your friends.

Ramen Hunting in Tokyo: Slurp down a proper ramen noodle bowl at a number of ramen shops. You'll know it's legit when you have to order at a machine first and hand over your ticket to the workers behind the counter.

Food Tour: Try taking a food tour one of your first days in Japan so you know what to look for during the rest of your stay. You'll leave full of knowledge and with a full belly.

Japan for the quirky traveler

There are endless weird and quirky things to do in Japan, so take full advantage of the culture.

Stay in a capsule hotel: Hope you're not claustrophobic. These hotels are more popular than you think and they are not that bad. Some have TV's and personal air conditioning.

Go to Comic Con in Japan: Time to get your geek on. Anime, superheroes and comic all together under one roof. If that's not quirky, then I don't know what is.

Take your picture in a photo booth: Not your average mall photo booth. Once you take fun pictures with your friends, head to the editing screen and make your eyes bigger, your cheeks blush, and your smile whiter. You can even add captions before it prints it out for you.

Vending Machine: Buy something completely random out of a vending machine, from socks to bread to headphones to beer.

Karaoke: Ah, a Japanese classic. Rent out a room with your friends and belt out your favorite 90's hits. Ben's is Wannabe by the Spice Girls.

Robot Restaurant Show: The most entertaining dinner you will ever go to. Lasers shining everywhere, robots battling right in front of you and dancers banging on drums, this show is unforgettable.

Japan for culture seekers

Stay at a Ryokan: Enjoy traditional Japanese hospitality in a paper-walled ryokan room while sleeping on a comfy futon on the ground. The service is always excellent and so are the meals.

Geisha Experience: Hang around the Gion district around dinner time in Kyoto to spot a geisha traveling to her events that evening. They typically don't like to be bothered so just watch from afar. You can attend a geisha performance, but be sure to.

Tea Ceremony: There is a specific art form to creating the perfect cup of tea and the Japanese have made that perfection. Probably the best cup of tea you'll ever have.

Temple Hopping: There are thousands of temples throughout Japan. Some in the heart of the city and others resting on the peaks of mountains. Try to understand the history of each temple you visit and awe in how many people they have served.

Responsible travel in Japan

Japan's super-efficient public transportation system makes it super easy to travel "green" in Japan, and this eco-friendly packing list that will help you travel sustainably.

If you would like to travel responsibly, here are a couple things to avoid in Japan:

Maid Cafe: this popular Tokyo cafe employs girls under the age of 18, and while it may seem innocent on the surface, a little digging will show you that these young women are exploited and sexualized for entertainment.

Animal Cafes: I 've been to a few dog and cat cafes in Korea, but have heard not so great things about the animal cafe culture in Japan when it comes to animals that are not typically domesticated, like owls and sheep. Again, do a little research and make your own informed decision about if you would like to support this business.

What to pack for your trip to Japan

When deciding what to pack for your trip to Japan, a big thing to consider is the time of year you will be visiting. In the wintertime, for instance, you will be encountering cold temperatures and will need warm clothing, whereas in summer the temperatures can be quite hot.

Here are some other items you'll want to consider packing for your trip to Japan:

Universal World Travel Adapter and Converter - This adaptor/converter can plug in to Japanese outlets (and over 150 other countries outlets) and convert the voltage to for you. No more shorting out your electronics.

Durable Backpack - I carry 40 liter backpacks everywhere I go.

Camera - You'll want to take lots of pictures!

Packing Cubes - A backpacking staple, these cubes help keep your clothes organized in your bag.

Microfiber Towel - Always good to carry around a fast drying microfiber towel just in case your hotel doesn't provide them.

Portable Battery Pack - It's the worst when you arrive to a new city and your phone is dead. Keep it charged with an Anker Battery Pack, this one can charge your phone up to 7 times.

Bamboo Sunglasses - Tree Tribe polarized sunglasses not only look great, but for every purchase they plant 10 trees.

Kindle Paperwhite - Download all your travel guidebooks onto your Kindle. You no longer have to carry around heavy books that take up space in your bag, and the Paperwhite version lights up in the dark.

Lush Solid Shampoo bar - No more worrying about liquid limits. One all-natural bar will last me up to 3 months and they smell great!

GoPro - One of the best ways to capture your travels. They are lightweight, take great pictures and video and they are waterproof up to 10 meters without a case!

Souvenir ideas in Japan

If you want to bring something special home from Japan, but don't want to resort to the typical, cliché items like shot glasses, key chains or magnets, here are some ideas for you!

Silk fan: With many beautiful designs to choose from, it may be hard to pick just one! Don't buy one from the first souvenir shop you see. Know that quality varies greatly, and some of the cheap ones may very well be made in China, so do some shopping around!

Ceramic tea set: Talk about a souvenir you'll appreciate for years to come. Can't pack a whole set? Why not pick up a couple beautiful tea cups. Just be sure you ask for them to be covered in bubble wrap!

Tea: If you're a tea lover, why not bring home some of the good stuff?! It is a practical souvenir and also makes a great gift.

Chopsticks: You can find beautiful chopsticks all around Japan. Some shops will even engrave your name on a set so that you always have "dibs"!

Ceramic vase: Find one at any craft market, perfect for a few flowers to brighten up a room.

Kimono: Get one that's comfortable and can be worn like a robe out of the shower! (Reminds of Schmidt from "New Girl"! Anyone else?)

Sake: Share a bottle or two with your friend back home to give them a taste of Japan.

Artwork: Bring home an art piece that will make you think of your time in Japan every time you look at it.

Calligraphy kit: Get your favorite quote done by a professional, or why not give it a go with your own set.

Cute things: Japan is full of Hello Kitty and all things cute. Pick up a small thing cutesy thing to bring back home with you.

Interesting foods: You'll find all sorts of "interesting" flavors of common snacks, like green tea flavored Kit Kats and sushi flavored Lays potato chips.

Daiso: If you're on a tight budget but want to pick up a souvenir (or 3!) head to Daiso, a Japanese "dollar store" that has super cute and random items that make great souvenirs on a budget.

Jobs for foreigners in Japan

If you've come to Japan, and just don't want to leave, there are a few ways you can extend your stay and make money or get compensated with room and board.

Teaching English: Similar to teaching English in South Korea, Japan has an organization call JET that places native English speakers in Japanese schools to teach English. And the pay is pretty good!

HelpX and WorkAway: Both are organizations that connect you with locals with business who need help in typically in exchange for room and board. Most of the jobs are in the hotel/guesthouse industry or English speaking services, but feel free to peek around.

VIPKID: If you want to truly make the most of your 90-day temporary tourist visa, but don't want to go broke, make some money on the side! Teaching English via video chat to children in China is a job where you can work from anywhere in the world, set your own hours and make great money! You can explore Japan during the day, and earn money in the evenings.

Around Japan

Tokyo

Yoking past and future, Tokyo dazzles with its traditional culture and passion for everything new.

Sci-fi cityscapes

Tokyo's neon-lit streetscapes still look like a sci-fi film set – and that's a vision of the city from the 1980s. Tokyo has been building ever since, pushing the boundaries of what's possible on densely populated, earthquake-prone land, adding ever taller, sleeker structures. Come see the utopian mega-malls, the edgy designer boutiques from Japan's award-winning architects, and the world's tallest tower – Tokyo Sky Tree – a twisting spire that draws on ancient building techniques. Stand atop one of Tokyo's skyscrapers and look out over the city at night to see it blinking like the control panel of a starship, stretching all the way to the horizon.

The shogun's city

Tokyo may be forever reaching into the future but you can still see traces of the shogun's capital on the kabuki stage, at a sumo tournament or under the cherry blossoms. It's a modern city built on old patterns, and in the shadows of skyscrapers you can find anachronistic wooden shanty bars and quiet alleys, raucous traditional festivals and lantern-lit yakitori (grilled chicken) stands. In older neighborhoods you can shop for handicrafts made just as they have been for centuries, or wander down cobblestone lanes where geisha once trod.

Eat your heart out

Yes, Tokyo has more Michelin stars than any other city. Yes, Japanese cuisine has been added to the UNESCO Intangible Cultural Heritage list. But that's not what makes dining in Tokyo such an amazing experience. What really counts is the city's long-standing artisan culture. You can splash out on the best sushi of your life, made by one of the city's legendary chefs using the freshest, seasonal market ingredients. You can also spend ¥800 on a bowl of noodles made with the same care and exacting attention to detail, from a recipe honed through decades of experience.

Fashion & pop culture

From giant robots to saucer-eyed schoolgirls to a certain, ubiquitous kitty, Japanese pop culture is a phenomenon that has reached far around the world. Tokyo is the country's pop-culture laboratory, where new trends grow legs. Come see the latest looks bubbling out of the backstreets of Harajuku, the hottest pop stars projected on the giant video screens in Shibuya, or the newest anime and manga flying off the shelves in Akihabara. Gawk at the giant statues of Godzilla; shop for your favorite character goods; or pick up some style inspiration just walking down the street.

Museums in Tokyo

Tokyo National Museum

Top choice museum in Ueno & Yanesen

Details:

13-9 Ueno-kōen

Taitō-ku

03-3822-1111

http://www.tnm.jp/

Hours: 9.30am-5pm Tue-Thu & Sun, to 9pm Fri & Sat

Price: adult/child & senior/student ¥620/free/410

If you visit only one museum in Tokyo, make it the Tokyo National Museum. Here you'll find the world's largest collection of Japanese art, including ancient pottery, Buddhist sculptures, samurai swords, colorful ukiyo-e (woodblock prints), gorgeous kimonos and much, much more. Visitors with only a couple of hours to spare should focus on the Honkan (Japanese Gallery) and the enchanting Gallery of Hōryū-ji Treasures, which displays masks, scrolls and gilt Buddhas from Hōryū-ji (in Nara Prefecture, dating from 607).

With more time, you can explore the three-storied Tōyōkan (Gallery of Asian Art), with its collection of Buddhist sculpture from around Asia and delicate Chinese ceramics. The Heiseikan, accessed via a passage on the 1st floor of the Honkan, houses the Japanese Archaeological Gallery, full of pottery, talismans and articles of daily life from Japan's prehistoric periods.

Check whether it's possible to access the usually off-limits garden, which includes several vintage teahouses; it opens to the public from mid-March to mid-April and from late October to early December.

The museum regularly hosts temporary exhibitions (which cost extra); these can be fantastic, but sometimes lack the English signage found throughout the rest of the museum.

Ghibli Museum

Top choice museum in West Tokyo

Details:

1-1-83 Shimo-Renjaku

Mitaka-shi

http://www.ghibli-museum.jp/

Hours: 10am-6pm, closed Tue

Price: adult ¥1000, child ¥100-700

Master animator Miyazaki Hayao, whose Studio Ghibli produced Princess Mononoke and Spirited Away, designed this museum. Fans will enjoy the original sketches; kids, even if they're not familiar with the movies, will fall in love with the fairy-tale atmosphere (and the big cat bus). Don't miss the original 20-minute animated short playing on the 1st floor.

Tickets must be purchased in advance, and you must choose the exact time and date you plan to visit.

Tickets can be purchased up to four months in advance from overseas travel agents or up to one month in advance through the convenience store Lawson's online ticket portal. Both options are explained in detail on the website. For July and August visits, I recommend buying tickets as soon as you can from an agent as they will definitely sell out early. Tickets are non-transferable; you may be asked to show an ID.

Getting to Ghibli (which is pronounced 'jiburi') is all part of the adventure. A minibus (round trip/one way ¥320/210) leaves for the museum every 20 minutes from Mitaka Station (bus stop 9). The museum is on the western edge of Inokashira-kōen, so you can also walk there through the park from Kichijōji Station in about 30 minutes.

Edo-Tokyo Museum

Top choice museum in Asakusa & Sumida River

Details:

1-4-1 Yokoami

Sumida-ku

03-3626-9974

http://www.edo-tokyo-museum.or.jp/

Hours: 9.30am-5.30pm, to 7.30pm Sat, closed Mon

Price: adult/child ¥600/free

Tokyo's history museum documents the city's transformation from tidal flatlands to feudal capital to modern metropolis via detailed scale recreations of townscapes, villas and tenement homes, plus artefacts such as ukiyo-e (woodblock prints) and old maps. Reopened in March 2018 after a renovation, the museum also has interactive displays, multilingual touch-screen panels, and audio guides. Still, the best way to tour the museum is with one of the gracious English-speaking volunteer guides, who can really bring the history to life.

There is a lot here and it would take a half-day to take it all in; if you're pressed for time, prioritize the section on Edo. A guide can also help steer you to the highlights. Skip the temporary exhibitions as they usually lack English (and the main exhibition is more than enough).

The museum is 62m tall – the same as height as the 17th-century keep at Edo-jō, the castle of the shogun – and the design, by Kiyonori Kikutake, is... something. The architect intended the structure to resemble a traditional raised-floor building in geometric abstraction. In reality, it looks a bit like an enormous concrete alien, in the style of the sprites from the video game Space Invaders.

Intermediatheque

Top choice museum in Marunouchi & Nihombashi

Details:

2nd & 3rd fl, JP Tower, 2-7-2 Marunouchi

Chiyoda-ku

03-5777-8600

http://www.intermediatheque.jp/

Hours: 11am-6pm, to 8pm Fri & Sat, usually closed on Sun & Mon

Dedicated to interdisciplinary experimentation, Intermediatheque cherry picks from the vast collection of the University of Tokyo (Tōdai) to craft a fascinating, contemporary museum experience. Go from viewing the best ornithological taxidermy collection in Japan to a giant pop-art print or the beautifully encased skeleton of a dinosaur. A handsome Tōdai lecture hall is reconstituted as a forum for events, including the playing of 1920s jazz recordings on a gramophone or old movie screenings.

Wandering in from the attached mall KITTE, you may think you've uncovered another high-concept boutique rather than this imaginatively designed, eclectic display of art, natural history and science treasures – that sense of disorientation and discovery is deliberate.

Ukiyo-e Ōta Memorial Museum of Art

Top choice museum in Harajuku & Aoyama

Details:

1-10-10 Jingūmae

Shibuya-ku

03-3403-0880

http://www.ukiyoe-ota-muse.jp/

Hours: 10.30am-5.30pm Tue-Sun

Price: adult ¥700-1000, child free

Change into slippers to enter the peaceful, hushed museum that houses the excellent ukiyo-e (woodblock prints) collection of Ōta Seizo, the former head of the Toho Life Insurance Company. Seasonal, thematic exhibitions are easily digested in an hour and usually include a few works by masters such as Hokusai and Hiroshige. It's often closed the last few days of the month.

The shop in the basement sells beautifully printed tenugui (traditional hand-dyed thin cotton towels).

Nezu Museum

Top choice museum in Harajuku & Aoyama

Details:

6-5-1 Minami-Aoyama

Minato-ku

03-3400-2536

Hours: 10am-5pm Tue-Sun

Price: adult/student/child ¥1100/800/free, special exhibitions extra ¥200

Nezu Museum offers a striking blend of old and new: a renowned collection of Japanese, Chinese and Korean antiquities in a gallery space designed by contemporary architect Kuma Kengo. Select items from the extensive collection are displayed in seasonal exhibitions. The English explanations are usually pretty good. Behind the galleries is a woodsy strolling garden laced with stone paths and studded with teahouses and sculptures.

There's a glass-walled cafe (also designed by Kuma), too.

National Museum of Modern Art (MOMAT)

Top choice museum in Marunouchi & Nihombashi

Details:

3-1 Kitanomaru-kōen

Chiyoda-ku

03-5777-8600

http://www.momat.go.jp/

Hours: 10am-5pm Tue-Thu, Sun, to 8pm Fri & Sat

Price: adult/student ¥500/250, 1st Sun of the month free

Regularly changing displays from the museum's superb collection of more than 12,000 works, by both local and international artists, are shown over floors two to four; special exhibitions are mounted on the ground floor. All pieces date from the Meiji period onward and impart a sense of how modern Japan has developed through portraits, photography, contemporary sculptures and video works. The museum closes in between exhibitions, so check the schedule online first.

Don't miss the 'Room with a View' for a panorama of the Imperial Palace East Garden. The museum also hosts excellent special exhibitions, which cost extra.

National Museum of Emerging Science & Innovation (Miraikan)

Top choice museum in Odaiba & Tokyo Bay

Details:

2-3-6 Aomi

Kōtō-ku

http://www.miraikan.jst.go.jp/

Hours: 10am-5pm Wed-Mon

Price: adult/child ¥620/210

Miraikan means 'hall of the future', and hands-on exhibits here present the science and technology that will (possibly!) shape the years to come. Don't miss the demonstrations of humanoid robot ASIMO (11am, 1pm, 2pm and 4pm) and the lifelike android Otonaroid (11.30am Monday and Wednesday to Friday, 11.30am and 2.30pm Saturday and Sunday). The Gaia dome theatre/planetarium (adult/child ¥300/100) has an English audio option and is popular; book online one week in advance. A multilingual smartphone app makes a game out of visiting.

Asakura Museum of Sculpture, Taitō

Top choice museum in Ueno & Yanesen

Details:

7-16-10 Yanaka

Taitō-ku

http://www.taitocity.net/taito/asakura

Hours: 9.30am-4.30pm Tue, Wed & Fri-Sun

Price: adult/child ¥500/250

Sculptor Asakura Fumio (artist name Chōso; 1883–1964) designed this atmospheric house himself. It combined his original Japanese home and garden with a large studio that incorporated vaulted ceilings, a 'sunrise room' and a rooftop garden with wonderful neighborhood views. It's now a reverential museum with many of the artist's signature realist works, mostly of people and cats, on display.

Shinto shrines in Tokyo

Meiji-jingū

Top choice shinto shrine in Harajuku & Aoyama

Details:

1-1 Yoyogi Kamizono-chō

Shibuya-ku

http://www.meijijingu.or.jp/

Hours: dawn-dusk

Tokyo's grandest Shintō shrine is dedicated to the Emperor Meiji and Empress Shōken, whose reign (1868–1912) coincided with Japan's transformation from isolationist, feudal state to modern nation. Constructed in 1920, the shrine was destroyed in WWII air raids and rebuilt in 1958; however, unlike so many of Japan's postwar reconstructions, Meiji-jingū has atmosphere in spades. Note that the shrine is currently undergoing renovations bit by bit in preparation for its 100th anniversary, but will remain open.

The main shrine is secreted in a wooded grove, accessed via a long winding gravel path. At the start of the path you'll pass through the first of several towering, wooden torii (gates). Just before the final torii is the temizu-ya (font), where visitors purify themselves by pouring water over their hands (purity is a tenet of Shintoism).

The main shrine, built of unpainted cypress wood, sparkles with a new copper-plated roof. To make an offering, toss a five-yen coin in the box, bow twice, clap your hands twice and then bow again. To the right of the main shrine, you'll see kiosks selling ema (wooden plaques on which prayers are written) and omamori (charms).

Time your visit for 8am or 2pm to catch the twice daily nikkusai, the ceremonial offering of food and prayers to the gods.

The shrine itself occupies only a small fraction of the sprawling forested grounds, which contain some 120,000 trees collected from all over Japan. Of this, only the strolling garden Meiji-jingū Gyoen is accessible to the public. The Meiji emperor himself designed the iris garden here to please the empress and the garden is most impressive when the irises bloom in June.

Hie-jinja

Shinto Shrine in Roppongi, Akasaka & Around

Details:

2-10-5 Nagatachō

Chiyoda-ku

03-3581-2471

http://www.hiejinja.net/

Hours: 5am-6pm Apr-Sep, 6am-5pm Oct-Mar

Enshrining the deity of sacred Mt Hiei, northeast of Kyoto, this hilltop shrine has been the protector shrine of Edo Castle, now the Imperial Palace, since it was first built in 1478. Host of one of Tokyo's three liveliest matsuri (festivals), Sannō-sai, it's an attractive place best approached by the tunnel of red torii (gates) on the hill's western side. There are also escalators up the hill from Tameike-sannō.

The shrine's present location dates from 1659, though it was destroyed in the 1945 bombings and rebuilt in 1967.

On the left, inside the main eastern entrance gate, the carved monkey clutching one of her young is emblematic of the shrine's ability to offer protection against the threat of a miscarriage.

Yasukuni-jinja

Shinto Shrine in Kōrakuen & Akihabara

Details:

3-1-1 Kudan-kita

Chiyoda-ku

03-3261-8326

http://www.yasukuni.or.jp/

Hours: 6am-5pm

Literally 'For the Peace of the Country Shrine', Yasukuni is the memorial shrine to Japan's war dead, around 2.5 million souls. First built in 1869, it is also incredibly controversial: in 1979, 14 class-A war criminals, including WWII general Hideki Tōjō, were enshrined here.

The main approach is fronted by a 25m-tall torii (entrance gate) made of steel and bronze; behind the main shrine, seek out the serene grove of mossy trees and the ornamental pond.

For politicians, a visit to Yasukuni, particularly on 15 August, the anniversary of Japan's defeat in WWII, is considered a political statement. It's a move that pleases hawkish constituents but also one that draws a strong rebuke from Japan's Asian neighbors, who suffered greatly in Japan's wars of expansion during the 20th century.

Architecture in Tokyo

Reversible Destiny Lofts

Details:

2-2-8 Ōsawa

Mitaka-shi

0422-26-4966

http://www.rdloftsmitaka.com/

Price: adult/child ¥2700/1000

Designed by husband and wife Arakawa Shūsaku (1936–2010) and Madeleine Gins (1941–2014) and completed in 2005, this housing complex certainly strikes against the mold: Created 'in memory of Helen Keller' the nine units have undulating, ridged floors, spherical dens and ceiling hooks for hammocks and swings. All this is meant to create a sensory experience beyond the visual (though the building is plenty colorful). Inside access is by tour only (check the website); the guides can speak some English.

Some units are occupied by residents, but others are available for short-term stays.

From JR Mitaka Station, take bus 51 or 52 (¥220, 15 minutes, every 10 to 15 minutes) from bus stop 2 on the station's south side and get off at Ōsawa Jūjiro (大沢十字路); you can see the building from the bus stop. Not all buses go this far, so show the driver where you want to go. Bus 1 (¥220, 25 minutes, every 10 to 15 minutes) goes here from Kichijōji Station (south exit, bus stop 3), alongside Inokashira-kōen.

Myōnichikan

Details:

2-31-3 Nishi-Ikebukuro

Toshima-ku

http://www.jiyu.jp/

Hours: 10am-4pm Tue-Sun

Price: with/without coffee ¥600/400

Lucky are the girls who attended the Frank Lloyd Wright–designed 'School of the Free Spirit' (Jiyū Gakuen; 自由学園). Built in 1921, Myōnichikan functioned as the school's main structure until the 1970s. After restoration, it was reopened as a public space in 2001. Visitors can tour the facilities and have coffee in the light-filled hall, sitting at low tables on (mostly) original chairs.

It can be tricky to find, though there are beige and green directional signs (in Japanese) on nearby utility poles.

Tokyo International Forum

Details:

3-5-1 Marunouchi

Chiyoda-ku

03-5221-9000

http://www.t-i-forum.co.jp/

Hours: 7am-11.30pm

This architectural marvel designed by Rafael Viñoly houses a convention and arts center, with eight auditoriums and a spacious courtyard in which concerts and events are held. The eastern wing looks like a glass ship plying the urban waters; you can access the catwalks from the 7th floor (take the lift).

Also visit for the twice-monthly Ōedo Antique Market and food trucks serving bargain meals and drinks to local office workers at lunch Monday to Friday.

Spiral Building

Details:

5-6-23 Minami-Aoyama

Minato-ku

03-3498-1171

http://www.spiral.co.jp/

Hours: 11am-8pm

The asymmetrical, geometric shape of architect Maki Fumihiko's Spiral Building (1985) may not look very sinuous on the outside, but the name will make more sense upon entry. The patchwork, uncentered design is a nod to Tokyo's own incongruous landscape. The spiraling passage inside doubles as an art gallery.

Check out the shop Spiral Market on the 2nd floor for art books, jewelry and stylish contemporary homewares.

Gardens in Tokyo

Rikugi-en

Top choice gardens in Ueno & Yanesen

Details:

6-16-3 Hon-Komgome

Bunkyō-ku

03-3941-2222

http://teien.tokyo-park.or.jp/en/rikugien

Hours: 9am-5pm

Price: adult/child/senior ¥300/free/150

Considered by many to be Tokyo's most elegant garden, Rikugi-en was originally completed in 1702, at the behest of a feudal lord. It is definitely the most highbrow, designed to evoke scenes from classical literature and mythology. But no context is necessary to appreciate the wooded walkways, stone bridges, central pond, trickling streams and wooden teahouses of this beautifully preserved garden. At one teahouse you can drink matcha (powdered green tea; ¥510) alfresco while overlooking the water.

There is almost always something in bloom at Rikugi-en, though the garden is most famous for its maple leaves in late autumn. Usually during late November and early December, the park stays open until 9pm and the trees are illuminated after sunset. In spring, the highlight is the large weeping cherry tree near the entrance.

Free, hour-long guided tours in English are offered at 11am and 2pm on the 1st and 3rd Sunday of the month.

Koishikawa Kōrakuen

Top choice gardens in Kōrakuen & Akihabara

Details:

1-6-6 Kōraku

Bunkyō-ku

03-3811-3015

http://teien.tokyo-park.or.jp/en/koishikawa

Hours: 9am-5pm

Price: adult/child ¥300/free

Established in the mid-17th century as the property of the Tokugawa clan, this formal strolling garden incorporates elements of Chinese and Japanese landscaping. It's among Tokyo's most attractive gardens, although nowadays the shakkei (borrowed scenery) also includes the other-worldly Tokyo Dome.

Don't miss the Engetsu-kyō (Full-Moon Bridge), which dates from the early Edo period (the name will make sense when you see it), and the beautiful vermilion wooden bridge Tsuten-kyō. The garden is particularly well known for its plum blossoms in February, irises in June and autumn leaves.

Hama-rikyū Onshi-teien

Top choice gardens in Ginza & Tsukiji

Details:

1-1 Hama-rikyū-teien

Chūō-ku

http://www.tokyo-park.or.jp/park/format/index028.html

Hours: 9am-5pm

Price: adult/child/senior ¥300/free/¥150

This beautiful garden, one of Tokyo's finest, is all that remains of a shogunate palace that once extended into the area now occupied by Tsukiji Market. The main features are a large duck pond with an island that's home to a charming tea pavilion, Nakajima no Ochaya, as well as some wonderfully manicured trees (black pine, Japanese apricot, hydrangeas etc.), some of which are hundreds of years old. Besides visiting the park as a side trip from Ginza or Tsukiji, consider travelling by boat to or from Asakusa via the Sumida-gawa (Sumida River).

Notable areas in Tokyo

Shimo-Kitazawa

Top choice area in Shibuya & Shimo-Kitazawa

Details:

Setagaya-ku

The narrow streets of 'Shimokita' are barely passable by cars, meaning a streetscape like a dollhouse version of Tokyo. It's been a favorite haunt of generations of students, musicians and artists. If hippies – not bureaucrats – ran Tokyo, the city would look a lot more like Shimo-Kitazawa. Although lacking big-name sights or landmarks, the neighborhood has a lively street scene all afternoon and evening, especially on weekends.

Restaurants, bars and entertainment venues are clustered on the south side; the more laid-back north side has many cafes and second-hand shops.

Omote-sandō

Top choice area in Harajuku & Aoyama

This regal, tree-lined boulevard was originally designed as the official approach to Meiji-jingū. Now it's a fashionable strip lined with high-end boutiques. Those designer shops come in designer buildings, which means Omote-sandō is one of the best places in the city to see contemporary architecture. Highlights include the Dior boutique by SANAA (Nishizawa Ryue and Sejima Kazuyo) and the Tod's boutique by Itō Toyō.

Galleries in Tokyo

Archi-Depot

Top choice gallery in Odaiba & Tokyo Bay

Details:

Warehouse Terrada, 2-6-10 Higashi-Shinagawa

Shinagawa-ku

03-5769-2133

http://archi-depot.com/

Hours: 11am-8pm Tue-Sun

Price: adult/student/child ¥2000/1000/free

This is brilliant: a facility that lets architects store the miniature models they make to conceptualize buildings (thus preserving them) and the public to see them up close. Many of the big names of Japanese architecture are represented here (Ban Shigero, Kuma Kengo). It looks very much like a storage room too, with the models sitting on rows of metal shelves (and not behind glass). Information about the architects can be accessed through QR codes.

Terrada Art Complex

Gallery in Odaiba & Tokyo Bay

Details:

3rd fl, 1-33-10 Higashi-Shinagawa

Shinagawa-ku

http://art.terrada.co.jp/

Hours: 11am-6pm Tue-Thu & Sat, to 8pm Fri

Part of the re-fashioning of the Tennōzu Isle warehouse district, this charcoal-grey warehouse contains six contemporary galleries: Kodama Gallery (www.kodamagallery.com), Urano (https://urano.tokyo/en), Yamamoto Gendai (www.yamamotogendai.org) and Yuka Tsuruno Gallery (http://yukatsuruno.com) on the 3rd floor and SCAI Park, a new space from SCAI the Bathhouse, and Kosaku Kanechika (http://kosakukanechika.com) on the 5th floor. Look for the English sign by the service elevator.

The elevator doors don't close by themselves; you'll need to press a button to close them manually after you exit (or else no one below can summon the elevator).

Origami Kaikan

Gallery in Kōrakuen & Akihabara

Details:

1-7-14 Yushima

Bunkyō-ku

03-3811-4025

http://www.origamikaikan.co.jp/

Hours: shop 9am-6pm, gallery 10am-5.30pm Mon-Sat

This exhibition center and workshop is dedicated to the quintessential Japanese art of origami, which you can learn to do yourself in classes here. There's a shop-gallery on the 1st floor, a gallery on the 2nd, and a workshop on the 4th where you can watch the process of making, dyeing and decorating origami paper.

Admission is free, but origami lessons (offered most days in Japanese) cost ¥1000 to ¥2500 for one to two hours, depending on the complexity of that day's design. First-timers would do well to try for a class with the centre's director, Kobayashi Kazuo.

Buddhist temples in Tokyo

Sensō-ji

Top choice Buddhist temple in Asakusa & Sumida River

Details:

2-3-1 Asakusa

Taitō-ku

03-3842-0181

http://www.senso-ji.jp/

Hours: 24hr

Tokyo's most visited temple enshrines a golden image of Kannon (the Buddhist goddess of mercy), which, according to legend, was miraculously pulled out of the nearby Sumida-gawa by two fishermen in AD 628. The image has remained on the spot ever since but is never on public display. The present structure dates from 1958. Entrance to the temple complex is via the fantastic, red Kaminari-mon (雷門; Thunder Gate) and busy shopping street Nakamise-dōri.

Before passing through the gate, look to either side to see statues of Fūjin (the god of wind) and Raijin (the god of thunder), and under the giant red lantern to see a beautiful carved dragon.

Stalls along Nakamise-dōri sell everything from tourist trinkets to genuine Edo-style crafts. At the end of Nakamise-dōri is the temple itself, and to your left you'll spot the 55m-high Five-Story Pagoda (五重塔). It's a 1973 reconstruction of a pagoda built by Tokugawa Iemitsu.

It's a mystery as to whether or not the ancient image of Kannon actually exists, as it's not on public display. This doesn't stop a steady stream of worshippers from visiting. In front of the temple is a large incense cauldron: the smoke is said to bestow health and you'll see people wafting it onto their bodies.

At the eastern edge of the temple complex is Asakusa-jinja, a shrine built in honor of the brothers who discovered the Kannon statue that inspired the construction of Sensō-ji. (Historically, Japan's two religions, Buddhism and Shintō, were intertwined and it was not uncommon for temples to include shrines and vice versa.) The current building, painted a deep shade of red, dates to 1649 and is a rare example of early Edo architecture. It's also the epicenter of one of Tokyo's most important festivals, May's Sanja Matsuri.

The entire temple complex is always busy, particularly so at weekends; consider visiting in the evening to see it with fewer people and the buildings beautifully illuminated.

Fukagawa Fudō-dō

Top choice Buddhist temple in Asakusa & Sumida River

Details:

1-17-13 Tomioka

Kōtō-ku

03-3630-7020

http://www.fukagawafudou.gr.jp/

Hours: 8am-6pm, to 8pm on festival days

Belonging to the esoteric Shingon sect, this is very much an active temple where you can attend one of the city's most spectacular religious rituals. Goma (fire rituals) take place daily in an auditorium in the Hondō (Main Hall) at 9am, 11am, 1pm, 3pm and 5pm, plus 7pm on festival days (1st, 15th and 28th of each month). Sutras are chanted, giant taiko drums are pounded and flames are raised on the main altar as an offering to the deity.

At the end of the 30-minute ceremony, people line up to have their bags and other possessions passed over the dying flames as a blessing.

While here, don't miss the trippy prayer corridor with 9500 miniature Fudōmyō (a fierce-looking representation of Buddha's determination) crystal statues. Upstairs is also a beautifully decorated gallery (open until 4pm) depicting all 88 temples of the 1400km pilgrimage route on the island of Shikoku; it is said that offering a prayer at each alcove has the same effect as visiting each temple.

Zōjō-ji

Buddhist Temple in Roppongi, Akasaka & Around

Details:

4-7-35 Shiba-kōen

Minato-ku

03-3432-1431

http://www.zojoji.or.jp/en/index.html

Hours: dawn-dusk

One of the most important temples of the Jōdō (Pure Land) sect of Buddhism, Zōjō-ji dates from 1393 and was the funerary temple of the Tokugawa regime. It's an impressive sight, particularly the main gate, Sangedatsumon, constructed in 1605, with its three sections designed to symbolize the three stages one must pass through to achieve nirvana. The Daibonsho (Big Bell; 1673) is a 15-tonne whopper considered one of the great three bells of the Edo period.

Like many sights in Tokyo, Zōjō-ji's original structures have been relocated, and were subject to war, fire and other natural disasters. It has been rebuilt several times in recent history, the last time in 1974.

On the temple grounds, there is a large collection of statues of the bodhisattva Jizō, said to be a guide during the transmigration of the soul, as well as a majestic Himalayan cedar planted by US president Ulysses S Grant in 1879.

Sengaku-ji

Buddhist Temple in Ebisu, Meguro & Around

Details:

2-11-1 Takanawa

Minato-ku

http://www.sengakuji.or.jp/

Hours: 7am-6pm Apr-Sep, to 5pm Oct-Mar

The story of the 47 rōnin (master less samurai) who avenged their master, Lord Asano – put to death after being tricked into pulling a sword on a rival – is legend in Japan. They were condemned to commit seppuku (ritual disembowelment) and their remains were buried at this temple. It's a somber place, with fresh incense rising from the tombs, placed there by visitors moved by the loyalty of the samurai. There is a small exhibition hall (adult/child ¥500/250) with artefacts and a video (available in English), which illustrate the story of the rōnin.

Parks in Tokyo

Yoyogi-kōen

Top choice park in Harajuku & Aoyama

Details:

http://www.yoyogipark.info/

If it's a sunny and warm weekend afternoon, you can count on there being a crowd lazing around the large grassy expanse that is Yoyogi-kōen. You can also usually find revelers and noisemakers of all stripes, from hula-hoopers to African drum circles to a group of retro greasers dancing around a boom box. It's an excellent place for a picnic and probably the only place in the city where you can reasonably toss a frisbee without fear of hitting someone.

During the warmer months, festivals take place on the plaza across from the park (see website, in Japanese, for a schedule). Cherry blossoms draw huge crowds and parties that go late into the night.

Shinjuku-gyoen

Top choice park in Shinjuku & Northwest Tokyo

Details:

11 Naito-chō

Shinjuku-ku

03-3350-0151

http://www.env.go.jp/garden/shinjukugyoen

Hours: 9am-4.30pm Tue-Sun

Price: adult/child ¥200/50

Though Shinjuku-gyoen was designed as an imperial retreat (completed 1906), it's now definitively a park for everyone. The wide lawns make it a favorite for urbanites in need of a quick escape from the hurly-burly of city life. Don't miss the greenhouse, with its giant lily pads and perfectly formed orchids, and the cherry blossoms in spring.

Inokashira-kōen

Park in West Tokyo

Details:

1-18-31 Gotenyama

Musashino-shi

http://www.kensetsu.metro.tokyo.jp/seibuk/inokashira/index.html

One of Tokyo's best parks, Inokashira-kōen has a big pond in the middle flanked by woodsy strolling paths. You can rent row boats (¥700 per hour) and swan-shaped pedal boats to take out onto the water (¥700 per 30 minutes). On weekends performance artists and craft vendors gather here (along with lots of Tokyoites of all ages). Don't miss the ancient shrine to the sea goddess Benzaiten and, in spring, the cherry blossoms.

To reach the park, walk straight from the Kōen exit of Kichijōji Station, cross at the light and veer right at Marui ('0101') department store; the park is at the end of the lane. Along the way, you'll pass shops selling takeaway items such as yakitori (grilled chicken skewers) and hot dogs.

Ueno-kōen

Park in Ueno & Yanesen

Details:

Ueno-kōen

Taitō-ku

http://ueno-bunka.jp/

Best known for its profusion of cherry trees that burst into blossom in spring (making this one of Tokyo's top hanami – blossom-viewing – spots), sprawling Ueno-kōen is also the location of the city's highest concentration of museums. At the southern tip is the large scenic pond, Shinobazu-ike, choked with lotus flowers in summer.

Navigating the park is easy, thanks to large maps in English. The wooded pathways also wind past centuries-old temples and shrines; the entire site was the domain of the temple Kanei-ji during the Edo era.

Gates in Tokyo

Kaminari-mon

Gate in Asakusa & Sumida River

Details:

2-3-1 Asakusa

Taitō-ku

The Sensō-ji temple precinct begins at this majestic gate, from which hangs an enormous chōchin (lantern); look under this to see a beautiful carved dragon. On either side are a pair of ferocious protective deities: Fūjin, the god of wind, on the right; and Raijin, the god of thunder, on the left. Kaminari-mon has burnt down countless times over the centuries; the current gate dates to 197.

Hōzō-mon

Gate in Asakusa & Sumida River

Details:

2-3-1 Asakusa

Taitō-ku

At the end of Sensō-ji's Nakamise-dōri, this gate is flanked by two fierce guardian deities. On the gate's back side are a pair of 2500kg, 4.5m-tall waraji (straw sandals) crafted for Sensō-ji by some 800 villagers in northern Yamagata Prefecture. These are meant to symbolize the Buddha's power, and it's believed that evil spirits will be scared off by the giant footwear.

Kuro-mon

Gate in Ueno & Yanesen

Details:

Tokyo National Museum, 13-9 Ueno-kōen

Taitō-ku

http://www.tnm.jp/

West of the main gate to Tokyo National Museum is the Kuro-mon (Black Gate), transported from the Edo-era mansion of a feudal lord. You can view the facade from outside the museum. On weekends, from 10am to 4pm, the gate is opened for visitors inside the museum to pass through.

Landmarks in Tokyo

Roppongi Hills

Top choice landmark in Roppongi, Akasaka & Around

Details:

6-chōme Roppongi

Minato-ku

http://www.roppongihills.com/

Hours: 11am-11pm

Roppongi Hills set the standard for 21st-century real-estate developments in Tokyo. The centerpiece of the office, shopping, dining and entertainment complex is the 54-storey Mori Tower, home to the Mori Art Museum and Tokyo City View observatory. Scattered around are several public artworks, such as Louise Bourgeois' giant, spiny Maman spider sculpture. There's also an Edo-style strolling garden, Mohri Garden.

The complex was designed by Jerde, a California-based, global pioneer of post-modern mall design. Japanese firm Maki and Associates did the Asahi TV building here.

Tokyo Station

Landmark in Marunouchi & Nihombashi

Details:

1-9 Marunouchi

Chiyoda-ku

http://www.tokyostationcity.com/

Tokyo Station celebrated its centenary in 2014 with a major renovation and expansion. Kingo Tatsuno's original elegant brick building on the Marunouchi side has been expertly restored to include domes faithful to the original design, decorated inside with relief sculptures. It's best viewed straight on from the plaza on Miyuki-dōri, the rooftop garden of the KITTE shopping mall, or the terrace on the 7th floor of the Shin-Maru Building. Tokyo Station Hotel occupies the south end of the building; to the north is Tokyo Station Gallery, which hosts interesting exhibitions, and the useful JR East Travel Service Center. Tokyo Station City, the name for the general nontransport complex, includes, on the eastern Yaesu side, Daimaru department store, and a vast and bewildering network of underground shopping and dining arcades. Here you can pick up a bentō (boxed lunch) – perfect for long train rides – and souvenirs from across Japan.

Tokyo Garden Terrace Kioi-chō

Landmark in Roppongi, Akasaka & Around

Details:

1-2 Kioi-chō

Chiyoda-ku

http://www.tgt-kioicho.jp/

This new mixed-use development is best visited for its pleasant surrounding gardens and public art, including White Deer by Nawa Kōhei and the giant metallic flowers of Ōmaki Shinji. Opened in 2016, on the former site of the Akasaka Grand Prince Hotel, the only piece remaining of the old complex is the restored Kitashirakawa Palace. Originally built in 1930 for the Korean Crown Prince Yi Un, this baronial-style mansion is now a restaurant and bar.

Also in the complex is the Prince Gallery Tokyo Kioi-chō hotel.

Restaurants in Tokyo

Kikunoi

Top choice kaiseki in Roppongi, Akasaka & Around

Details:

6-13-8 Akasaka

Minato-ku

03-3568-6055

http://kikunoi.jp/

Hours: noon-1pm Tue-Sat, 5-8pm Mon-Sat

Price: lunch/dinner course from ¥11,900/19,000

Exquisitely prepared seasonal dishes are as beautiful as they are delicious at this Tokyo outpost of one of Kyoto's most acclaimed kaiseki (Japanese haute cuisine) restaurants. Kikunoi's third-generation chef, Murata Yoshihiro, has written a book translated into English on kaiseki that the staff helpfully use to explain the dishes you are served, if you don't speak Japanese. Reservations are necessary.

Kyūbey

Sushi in Ginza & Tsukiji

Details:

8-7-6 Ginza

Chūō-ku

03-3571-6523

http://www.kyubey.jp/

Hours: 11.30am-2pm & 5-10pm Mon-Sat

Price: lunch/dinner set from ¥4320/11,880

Since 1935, Kyūbey's quality and presentation has won it a moneyed and celebrity clientele. Even so, this is a supremely open and relaxed restaurant. The friendly owner Imada-san speaks excellent English as do some of his team of talented chefs, who will make and serve your sushi, piece by piece. The ¥8000 lunchtime omakase (chef's selection) is great value.

Lunch reservations are accepted only for the 11.30am seating; otherwise you can queue for a spot. For a real treat at dinner, order the kaiseki (Japanese haute cuisine) menu (¥31,500) served on pottery by famed artisan Kitaoji Rosanjin. There's an exhibition of Rosanjin pieces on the restaurant's 4th floor.

Innsyoutei

Japanese in Ueno & Yanesen

Details:

4-59 Ueno-kōen

Taitō-ku

03-3821-8126

http://www.innsyoutei.jp/

Hours: restaurant 11am-3pm & 5-9.30pm, tearoom 11am-5pm

Price: lunch/dinner from ¥1680/5500

In a gorgeous wooden building dating back to 1875, Innsyoutei (pronounced 'inshotei' and meaning 'rhyme of the pine cottage') has long been a favorite spot for fancy kaiseki-style meals while visiting Ueno-kōen. Without a booking (essential for dinner) you'll have a long wait but it's worth it. Lunchtime bentō (boxed meals) offer beautifully presented morsels and are great value.

There's an attached rustic teahouse serving matcha (powdered green tea) and traditional desserts from ¥600.

Sougo

Vegetarian in Roppongi, Akasaka & Around

Details:

3rd fl, Roppongi Green Bldg, 6-1-8 Roppongi

Minato-ku

03-5414-1133

http://www.sougo.tokyo/

Hours: 11.30am-3pm & 6-11pm Mon-Sat

Price: set lunch/dinner from ¥1500/6500

Sit at the long counter beside the open kitchen or in booths and watch the expert chefs prepare delicious and beautifully presented shōjin-ryōri (vegetarian cuisine as served at Buddhist temples). Lunch is a bargain. Reserve at least one day in advance if you want them to prepare a vegan meal. Look for it in the building opposite the APA Hotel.

Also here is Tokyo Cook, offering a variety of Japanese cooking classes in English.

Tonki'

Tonkatsu in Ebisu, Meguro & Around

Details:

1-2-1 Shimo-Meguro

Meguro-ku

03-3491-9928

Hours: 4-10.45pm Wed-Mon, closed 3rd Mon of the month

Price: meals ¥1900

Tonki is a Tokyo tonkatsu (crumbed pork cutlet) legend, deep-frying pork cutlets, recipe unchanged, for nearly 80 years. The seats at the counter – where you can watch the perfectly choreographed chefs – are the most coveted, though there is usually a queue. There are tables upstairs.

From the station, walk down Meguro-dōri, take a left at the first alley and look for a white sign and noren (doorway curtains) across the sliding doors.

Maisen

Tonkatsu in Harajuku & Aoyama

Details:

4-8-5 Jingūmae

Shibuya-ku

http://mai-sen.com/

Hours: 11am-10pm

Price: lunch/dinner from ¥995/1680

You could order something else (maybe fried shrimp), but everyone else will be ordering the famous tonkatsu (breaded, deep-fried pork cutlets). There are different grades of pork on the menu, including prized kurobuta (black pig), but even the cheapest is melt-in-your-mouth divine. The restaurant is housed in an old public bathhouse. A takeaway window (10am to 7pm) serves delicious tonkatsu sando (sandwich).

Tofuya-Ukai

Kaiseki in Roppongi, Akasaka & Around

Details:

4-4-13 Shiba-kōen

Minato-ku

03-3436-1028

http://www.ukai.co.jp/english/shiba

Hours: 11am-10pm, last order 8pm

Price: lunch/dinner set menu from ¥6500/11,900

One of Tokyo's most gracious restaurants is located in a former sake brewery (moved from northern Japan), with an exquisite traditional garden, in the shadow of Tokyo Tower. Seasonal preparations of tofu and accompanying dishes are served in the refined kaiseki style. Make reservations well in advance. Vegetarians should tell the staff when they book.

Kizushi

Sushi in Marunouchi & Nihombashi

Details:

2-7-13 Nihombashi Ningyōchō

Chūō-ku

03-3666-1682

Hours: 11.45am-2.30pm Mon-Sat, 5-9.30pm Mon-Fri

Price: lunch/dinner course from ¥3500/10,000

While sushi has moved in the direction of faster and fresher, Kizushi, in business since 1923, is keeping it old-school. Third generation chef Yui Ryuichi uses traditional techniques, such as marinating the fish in salt or vinegar, from back when sushi was more about preservation than instant gratification. The shop is in a lovely old timber-frame house. Reservations required for dinner.

Ginza Kagari'

Ramen in Ginza & Tsukiji

Details:

Basement, Echika Fit, 4-1-2 Ginza

Chūō-ku

03-3561-0717

Hours: 11am-11pm

Price: small/large ramen ¥950/1050

Kagari, currently one of Tokyo's most-obsessed-about ramen shops, does a luscious tori paitan (fat-rich chicken broth) topped with delicately steamed seasonal vegetables – it will make you rethink ramen. While the main shop moves to a new location, visit this branch in the Echika Fit underground arcade in Ginza station. There's only eight seats so expect a queue.

d47 Shokudō

Japanese in Shibuya & Shimo-Kitazawa

Details:

8th fl, Shibuya Hikarie, 2-21-1 Shibuya

Shibuya-ku

http://www.hikarie8.com/d47shokudo/about.shtml

Hours: 11am-2.30pm & 6-10.30pm

Price: meals ¥1200-1780

There are 47 prefectures in Japan and d47 serves a changing line-up of teishoku (set meals) that evoke the specialties of each, from the fermented tofu of Okinawa to the stuffed squid of Hokkaido. A larger menu of small plates is available in the evening. Picture windows offer bird's-eye views over the trains coming and going at Shibuya Station.

Tempura Kondō

Tempura in Ginza & Tsukiji

Details:

Sakaguchi Bldg 9th fl, 5-5-13 Ginza

Chūō-ku

03-5568-0923

Hours: noon-3pm, 5-10pm Mon-Sat

Price: lunch/dinner course from ¥7000/12,000

Nobody in Tokyo does tempura vegetables like chef Kondo Fumiō. The carrots are julienned to a fine floss; the corn is pert, juicy; and the sweet potato is comfort food at its finest. Courses include seafood too, picked up that morning from Tsukiji. Lunch service at noon or 1.30pm; last dinner booking at 8.30pm. Reserve ahead.

Shirube

Izakaya in Shibuya & Shimo-Kitazawa

Details:

2-18-2 Kitazawa

Setagaya-ku

03-3413-3785

Hours: 5.30pm-midnight

Price: dishes ¥430-1060

It's a tossup as to which has the most character here: the inventive fusion dishes or the charismatic staff who put on a show in the open kitchen. Either way, Shirube is among Tokyo's most beloved izakaya. Don't miss the aburi saba (blow-torch grilled mackerel), the house specialty. Reservations recommended (and a must on weekends); cover charge ¥400 per person. Heading down the hill from Shimo-Kitazawa Station's south exit, make a right in front of Mr. Donuts and look for the white noren (doorway curtains) on your right.

Daiwa Sushi

Sushi in Ginza & Tsukiji

Details:

Bldg 6, 5-2-1 Tsukiji

Chūō-ku

03-3547-6807

Hours: 5.30am-1.30pm Mon, Tue & Thu-Sat

Price: sushi set ¥3780

Waits of over one hour are commonplace at Tsukiji Market's most famous sushi bar, after which you'll be expected to eat and run. But it's all worth it once your first piece of delectable sushi hits the counter. Unless you're comfortable ordering in Japanese, the standard set (seven nigiri, plus maki and miso soup) is a good bet; there's a picture menu.

Until the market move to Toyosu in 2017 (or later), Daiwa Sushi is located within the jōnai-shijō (inner market) of Tsukiji Market.

Tensuke

Tempura in West Tokyo

Details:

3-22-7 Kōenji-kita

Suginami-ku

03-3223-8505

Hours: noon-2pm & 6-10pm Tue-Sun

Price: lunch/dinner from ¥1100/1600

An entirely legitimate candidate for eighth wonder of the modern world is Tensuke's tamago (egg) tempura. I don't know how the chef (who is quite a showman) does it, but the egg comes out batter-crisp on the outside and runny in the middle. It's served on rice with seafood and vegetable tempura as part of the tamago tempura teishoku (玉子天ぷら定食).

There's a blue and orange sign out front; expect to queue.

Onigiri Yadoroku

Japanese in Asakusa & Sumida River

Details:

3-9-10 Asakusa

Taitō-ku

03-3874-1615

http://onigiriyadoroku.com/

Hours: 11.30am-5pm Mon-Sat, 6pm-2am Thu-Tue

Price: set lunch ¥660 & ¥900, onigiri ¥200-600

Onigiri (rice-ball snacks), usually wrapped in crispy sheets of nori (seaweed), are a great Japanese culinary invention. And they're not just convenience store snacks: try them fresh at Tokyo's oldest onigiri shop, which feels more like a sushi counter. The set lunches are a great deal; at night there's a large range of flavors to choose from, along with alcohol.

Harajuku Gyōza-rō

Dumplings in Harajuku & Aoyama

Details:

6-4-2 Jingūmae

Shibuya-ku

Hours: 11.30am-4.30am, to 10pm Sun

Price: 6 gyōza ¥290

Gyōza (dumplings) are the only thing on the menu here, but you won't hear any complaints from the regulars who queue up to get their fix. Have them sui (boiled) or yaki (pan-fried), with or without niniku (garlic) or nira (chives) – they're all delicious. Expect to wait on weekends or at lunchtime, but the line moves quickly.

Asakusa Imahan

Japanese in Asakusa & Sumida River

Details:

3-1-12 Nishi-Asakusa

Taitō-ku

03-3841-1114

http://www.asakusaimahan.co.jp/

Hours: 11.30am-9.30pm

Price: lunch/dinner set menu from ¥4000/10,000

For a meal to remember, swing by this famous beef restaurant, in business since 1895. Choose between courses of sukiyaki (sautéed beef dipped in raw egg) and shabu-shabu (beef blanched in broth); Prices rise according to the grade of meat. For diners on a budget, Imahan sells a limited number of cheaper lunch sets (from ¥1620).

Dhaba India

South Indian in Marunouchi & Nihombashi

Details:

2-7-9 Yaesu

Chūō-ku

03-3272-7160

http://dhabaindia.com/dhaba/index.html

Hours: 11.15am-3pm & 5-11pm Mon-Fri, noon-3pm & 5-10pm Sat & Sun

Price: lunch from ¥850, mains from ¥1370

Indian meals in Tokyo don't come much better than those served at this long-established restaurant with deep-indigo plaster walls. The food is very authentic, particularly the curries served with basmati rice, naan or crispy dosa (giant lentil-flour pancakes). Set lunches are spectacularly good value.

Honmura-An

Soba in Roppongi, Akasaka & Around

Details:

7-14-18 Roppongi

Minato-ku

03-5772-6657

http://www.honmuraantokyo.com/

Hours: noon-2.30pm & 5.30-10pm Tue-Sun, closed 1st & 3rd Tue of the month

Price: noodles from ¥900; set lunch/dinner ¥1600/7400

This fabled soba shop, once located in Manhattan, now serves its handmade buckwheat noodles at this rustically contemporary noodle shop on a Roppongi side street. The delicate flavor of these noodles is best appreciated when served on a bamboo mat, with tempura or with dainty slices of kamo (duck).

Activities in Tokyo

Mt. Fuji, Lake Ashi and Bullet Train Day Tour from Tokyo

From $141

Duration: 11 hours

Departure/Return:

Ginza Pickup: Courtyard by Marriott Tokyo Ginza Hotel Ikebukuro Pickup: Hotel Metropolitan (Tokyo Ikebukuro) Hamamatsucho Bus Terminal Pickup: Hamamatsucho Bus Terminal Shinagawa Pickup: Grand Prince Hotel New Takanawa (in Shinagawa) Shinjuku Pickup: Keio Plaza Hotel Tokyo (in Shinjuku) - The tour concludes at Shin-Yokohama Station, Shinagawa Station, or Tokyo Station around 8:00pm

Discover some of Japan's most famous highlights on a full-day guided tour from Tokyo. Travel to Mt Fuji's bustling 5th Station and learn about the revered mountain. Continue to nearby Lake Ashi for a short boat cruise, followed by a ride on the Mt Komagatake Ropeway. Climb by aerial tram to the top of Mt Komagatake and get fantastic views of the Owakudani volcanic valley, Lake Ashi and Mt Fuji. Return to Tokyo by bullet train in the evening. Enjoy the ease of included transportation, entry fees and a knowledgeable guide.

After morning pickup at select hotels or designated meeting location in Tokyo, relax as your deluxe coach cruises along a scenic 2.5-hour route to Mt Fuji Visitor Center. Learn about the history and geology of Japan's highest mountain from your guide and the informational exhibits about the revered mountain. From the second floor observation deck, you can get great views of Mt Fuji on a clear day. After seeing the Visitor Center, return to your coach and proceed to Mt Fuji's 5th Station, located about halfway up the mountain at 7,545 feet (2,300m). Take in the shrines, torii gates and shops that sell souvenirs, along with views of Mt Fuji and the surrounding lakes (subject to weather conditions). Soak in the invigorating atmosphere of 5th Station; you might even spot some climbers preparing for their adventure. Then have time to enjoy Japanese-style lunch (if you select the "+ Lunch" option at checkout). Otherwise, you have the option to buy your own meal. After having a bite to eat, drive to nearby Lake Ashi, located in Hakone National Park. Step aboard your boat for a short cruise across the lake. Admire the spectacular scenery of pristine waters surrounded by Mt Komagatake, Mt Fuji and other mountains. Disembark from the boat and head to the Mt Komagatake Ropeway, an aerial tram that takes you from the shores of Lake Ashi to the top of Mt Komagatake. Have time to walk around the mountain top and take in amazing views of Lake Ashi, the Owakudani volcanic valley and majestic Mt Fuji. After visiting Hakone, transfer by coach to the evening bullet train (Shinkansen) for your return to Tokyo, where your guide will tell you how to get back to your hotel. Please note: Views around Mt Fuji are always subject to weather conditions as mountain weather is notoriously unpredictable. Visibility tends to be better during the colder months, in the early morning and late evening.

What's included:

One-way bus ride

One-way bullet train (Shinkansen) ride to Tokyo Station

Pickup at select hotels and locations in Tokyo (see Departure Point for Details:)

Free Wi-Fi access on bus

Lunch (only if you select "+ Lunch" option at checkout)

Entrance fees

Professional guide

Cruise on Lake Ashi

Mt. Komagatake Ropeway

What's not included

Gratuities (optional)

Hotel drop-off

Drinks

Highlights

Instant Confirmation

Day trip (destination A to B)

Informative, friendly and professional guide

Travel by boat and see the sights from the water

All entrance fees included

Hotel pickup included

Tokyo 1-Day Tour: Meiji Shrine, Asakusa Temple, Bay Cruise

From $90

Duration: 8.5 hours

Departure/Return:

ANA InterContinental Tokyo Cerulean Tower Tokyo Hotel Courtyard by Marriott Tokyo Ginza Hotel Dai-ichi Hotel Tokyo Ginza Capital Hotel Annex Gotanda Station West Exit Grand Hyatt Tokyo Grand Prince Hotel New Takanawa Hamamatsucho Bus Terminal Hilton Tokyo Hotel Grand Palace Hotel Metropolitan Tokyo Ikebukuro Hotel New Otani Tokyo Hotel Okura Tokyo Hyatt Regency Tokyo Imperial Hotel, Tokyo Keio Plaza Hotel Tokyo Park Hotel Tokyo Sheraton Miyako Hotel Tokyo Shiba Park Hotel Shinagawa Prince Hotel Shinjuku Station East Exit Shinjuku Washington Hotel Main Sunshine City Prince Hotel The New Sanno Tokyo City Air Terminal Tokyo Dome Hotel Tokyo Station Marunouchi South Exit - Tokyo Station's Marunouchi South Exit (approximately 5:30pm)

Discover the highlights of Tokyo on a full-day guided tour, the perfect introduction to the city. Visit Meiji Shrine, Japan's most famous Shinto shrine, stroll the gardens of the Imperial Palace, and spend time at Asakusa Kannon Temple (Senso-ji), Tokyo's oldest Buddhist temple. See shopping areas like Nakamise Shopping Street and the Ginza district, then enjoy a boat cruise on Tokyo Bay. Your experienced guide shares the history and culture of Tokyo as you explore the ancient and modern aspects of this bustling city.

After morning pickup from selected hotels, travel by comfortable coach to the Meiji Shrine, which was dedicated to the Emperor and Empress in 1926. Hear from your guide why the Meiji Shrine is Tokyo's most popular and important Shinto shrine while you stroll around the buildings and gardens. Return to the coach and drive past the towering Japanese House of Parliament en route to the Imperial Palace East Garden. Located outside the Imperial Palace on the grounds of a former Edo-era castle, the expansive grounds contain a tea pavilion, traditional Japanese garden, a moat and stone walls. Next, walk along Nakamise Shopping Street, a colorful promenade lined with food stands and souvenir shops that leads up to Tokyo's oldest and most significant Buddhist temple, Asakusa Kannon Temple (also known as Senso-ji). Your guide takes you through the market to tour the magnificent architecture, shrines, and Japanese gardens around the temple. Leave Asakusa Kannon Temple and drive by the celebrated Ginza shopping district with its eye-popping neon lights, department stores and giant theaters. Then sit down for a Western-style lunch at Pastel-Tei restaurant, which overlooks Hamarikyu Garden, Tokyo's only surviving seaside garden from the Edo period. (In 2017, you'll head to Yurakucho to join a traditional Japanese dance activity before enjoying a lunch buffet.) When you finish your meal, board a large boat for a 1-hour cruise around Tokyo Bay. Snap photos of Tokyo's skyline and iconic sights such as Rainbow Bridge. At the end of your cruise, check out the futuristic waterfront shopping district called Aqua City Odaiba. Keep an eye out for architectural fancies in this area, including the Fuji TC Building, Tokyo Big Sight, and Telecom Center. Your tour ends at Tokyo Station as you make your own way to your hotel. Please note: On Mondays, Fridays and other days when the Imperial Palace East Garden is closed, you will visit Imperial Palace Plaza instead.

What's included:

Tokyo Bay cruise

Transport by air-conditioned coach

Professional guide

Entrance fees

Lunch

Hotel pickup (select hotels in Tokyo only)

What's not included

Drinks

Gratuities (optional)

Highlights

Instant Confirmation

Perfect introduction for first-time visitors

Comprehensive tour by bus/coach

Travel by boat and see the sights from the water

Informative, friendly and professional guide

All entrance fees included

Hotel pickup included

Tokyo Robot Cabaret Evening Show Ticket

Food, Wine & Nightlife in Tokyo

From £49.61

More info

Duration: 1.5 hours

Departs: Robot Restaurant

Prepare for an eclectic evening with a Japanese cabaret show at the Robot Restaurant in Tokyo's Kabukicho red-light district! Each entertaining 1-hour show features fun – and sometimes campy – performances full of flashing lights, taiko drums and techno music. See glitzy girls dance with a giant panda, dinosaurs, ninjas and (of course) robots on stage! Your entry ticket includes one drink of your choice (beer, sake, mineral water or soft drink).

Arrive 40 minutes early at the Robot Restaurant in the red-light district of Kabukicho for your show (time depending on the option selected). After checking in and selecting a drink, wait in the lounge until you are escorted to your seat for the evening entertainment known as the robot cabaret. Watch in amazement as neon tanks come out to battle alongside Godzilla, robots, samurais and ninjas. Dancing girls in colorful outfits join dinosaurs and pandas on stage against a backdrop of video screens. Flashing lights, accompanied by taiko drums and loud techno-style music, illuminate the performance of massive female robots – truly a spectacle not to be missed! Revel in this one-of-a-kind cabaret show for about one hour and enjoy a drink of your choice. Drinks include draft beer, canned beer, sake, canned alcopops, mineral water and various soft drinks. (Additional beverages available for purchase.) You'll have plenty to rave about at the end of this highly entertaining musical show!

What's included:

Admission ticket

1 complimentary drink

What's not included

Hotel pickup and drop-off

Additional food and drink orders

Highlights

Likely to Sell Out

Several menus to choose from

Multiple times offered throughout the day

Free drinks included

Tokyo Sumo Wrestling Tournament

Cultural & theme tours in Tokyo

From $86

Duration: 5 hours

Departure/Return:

Hamamatsucho Bus Terminal or Ryogoku View Hotel (near Ryogoku Sumo Hall) - If you select the tour option "No Dinner", the tour concludes at the stadium. If you select the tour option "Dinner Included", the tour concludes at the restaurant near the stadium

Don't miss the opportunity to see a traditional sumo tournament when you're in Tokyo. Ride the subway with fellow sumo fans to the 'kokugikan' (sumo amphitheater) and enjoy several sumo-wrestling matches in the afternoon. Beforehand, visit the fascinating Sumo Museum to see sumo-related objects from the Edo period to the present. Upgrade your experience to include dinner at a chanko restaurant with delicious Japanese stew.

Meet your group at Hamamatsucho Bus Terminal or Ryogoku View Hotel (near the stadium) in the afternoon, and head to Ryogoku Sumo Hall. Stop by the Sumo Museum where you can learn about this 1,500-year-old Japanese cultural tradition before you continue to the arena to watch the real thing. See important sumo-related items on display, such as woodblock prints, folding screens and ceremonial aprons from as far back as the Edo period. Next head into the Grand Sumo Tournament at Ryogoku Kokugikan. Feel the excitement during an opening ceremony called dohyo-iri, where your guide will start to explain what's happening at the amphitheater. You'll watch a series of sumo wrestlers grapple in the elevated ring — made of clay and covered in a layer of sand — from your B-class reserved seat on the second floor. Consult your brochure and sumo-ranking list for the day's events; junior division sumo matches are held first, proceeding the higher-ranked matches slated for later in the day. Another way you'll know when the big matches are on: the makuuchi (senior-division wrestlers) wear kesho-mawashi, or ceremonial apron. Put on your headphones and listen to English commentary throughout the approximate 2.5-hour match, following along during each lightning-speed match of one minute or less. Watching the sumo matches is the main event, but there are other things to enjoy at the arena. Check out the championship flags in the entrance lobby, purchase a bite to eat from one of the vendors at any time, and don't forget to browse the various sumo-related goods on sale. Afterward, your guide accompanies you to Hamamatsucho Bus Terminal and explains directions back to your hotel. If you select the dinner option, you're taken to a nearby restaurant. Optional Upgrade: Dinner Upgrade your experience to include dinner at a local chanko or sukiyaki restaurant, most likely run by a former sumo wrestler. Enjoy chankonabe, a hearty stew that is the traditional food of sumo wrestler, or sukiyaki, a dish consisting of thin slices of meat, tofu, and vegetables cooked in a soy sauce-based broth. Your guide will not join you for dinner, leaving you to make your own way back to your hotel.

What's included:

B-Class arena chair seat on the second floor

Professional guide

Sumo information pamphlet and sumo-ranking list (in English)

Dinner (only if "Dinner Included" option is selected)

What's not included

Hotel pickup/drop-off

Gratuities (optional)

Highlights

Likely to Sell Out

All entrance fees included

When to go and weather

Spring and autumn are the best times to visit: spring has cherry blossoms; autumn has arts events. Mid-June to mid-July is the rainy season; August is hot and humid, but is also the month for summer festivals.

Tokyo month by month

Top Events

Hatsu-mōde, January

Cherry Blossoms, April

Sanja Matsuri, May

Sumida-gawa Fireworks, July

Kōenji Awa Odori, August

January

Tokyo comes to a halt for O-shōgatsu, the first three days of the new year set aside for family and rest; most places close and many residents return to their home towns.

Hatsu-mōde

Hatsu-mōde, the first shrine visit of the new year, starts just after midnight on 1 January and continues through O-shōgatsu. Meiji-jingū is the most popular spot in Tokyo; it can get very, very crowded, but that's part of the experience.

Emperor's New Year Greeting

On the morning of 2 January, the emperor makes a brief – and rare – public appearance in an inner courtyard of the Imperial Palace; the same ceremonial greeting is also held on 23 December, the emperor's birthday.

Coming of Age Day

The second Monday of January is seijin-no-hi, the collective birthday for all who have turned 20 (the age of majority) in the past year; young women don gorgeous kimonos for ceremonies at Shintō shrines.

February

February is the coldest month, though it rarely snows. Winter days are crisp and clear – the best time of year to spot Mt Fuji in the distance.

Setsubun

The first day of spring is 3 February in the traditional lunar calendar, a shift once believed to bode evil. As a precaution, people visit Buddhist temples, toss roasted beans and shout, 'Oni wa soto! Fuku wa uchi!' ('Devil out! Fortune in!').

Shimo-Kitazawa Tengu Matsuri

On the weekend nearest to Setsubun (late January or early February), Shimo-Kitazawa hosts a parade with revelers dressed in tengu (devil) costumes.

Plum Blossoms

Plum (ume) blossoms, which appear towards the end of the month, are the first sign that winter is ending. Popular viewing spots include Koishikawa Kōrakuen and Yushima Tenjin.

March

Hina Matsuri

On and around 3 March (also known as Girls' Day), public spaces and homes are decorated with o-hina-sama (princess) dolls in traditional royal dress.

Anime Japan

In late March, Anime Japan has events and exhibitions for industry insiders and fans alike, at Tokyo Big Sight.

April

Warmer weather and blooming cherry trees make this quite simply the best month to be in Tokyo.

Cherry Blossoms

From the end of March through the beginning of April, the city's parks and riversides turn pink and Tokyoites toast spring in spirited parties, called hanami, beneath the blossoms. Ueno-kōen is the most famous spot, but grassy Yoyogi-kōen and Shinjuku-gyoen are more conducive to picnicking.

Hana Matsuri

In honor of the Buddha's birthday on 8 April, Hana Matsuri (flower festival) celebrations take place at temples. Look for the parade of children in Asakusa, pulling a white papier-mâché elephant.

May

There's a string of national holidays at the beginning of May, known as Golden Week, when much of the country makes travel plans. Festivals and warm days make this an excellent time to visit.

Children's Day

On 5 May, also known as otoko-no-hi (Boys' Day), families fly koinobori (colorful banners in the shape of a carp), a symbol of strength and courage.

Tokyo Rainbow Pride

In May, Japan's LGBT community comes together for the country's biggest pride event (http://tokyorainbowpride.com), in some years followed by a parade. It's not London or Sydney, but a spirited affair just the same.

Kanda Matsuri

This is one of Tokyo's big three festivals, with a parade of mikoshi (portable shrines) around Kanda Myōjin. It's held on the weekend closest to 15 May on odd-numbered years (next up 2019).

Design Festa

Weekend-long Design Festa, held at Tokyo Big Sight in mid-May, is Asia's largest art festival, featuring performances and thousands of exhibitors.

Sanja Matsuri

Arguably the grandest Tokyo matsuri (festival) of all, this three-day event, held over the third weekend of May, attracts around 1.5 million spectators to Asakusa-jinja. The highlight is the rowdy parade of mikoshi carried by men and women in traditional dress.

Roppongi Art Night

Held in mid- to late October, this weekend-long (literally, as venues stay open all night) arts event (www.roppongiartnight.com) sees large-scale installations and performances taking over the streets of Roppongi.

June

Early June is lovely, though by the end of the month tsuyu (the rainy season) sets in.

Sannō Matsuri

For a week in mid-June Hie-jinja puts on this major festival, with music, dancing and a procession of mikoshi. The parade takes place in even-numbered years.

July

When the rainy season passes in mid- to late July, suddenly it's summer – the season for lively street fairs and hanabi taikai (fireworks shows).

Tanabata

On 7 July, the stars Vega and Altar (stand-ins for a princess and cowherd who are in love) meet across the Milky Way. Children tie strips of coloured paper bearing wishes around bamboo branches; look for decorations at youthful hang-outs such as Harajuku and Shibuya.

Mitama Matsuri

Yasukuni-jinja celebrates O-Bon early: from 13 to 16 July, the shrine holds a festival of remembrance for the dead with 30,000 illuminated bonbori (paper lanterns).

Ueno Natsu Matsuri

From mid-July to mid-August various events, including markets and music performances, take place in Ueno-kōen.

Sumida-gawa Fireworks

The grandest of the summer fireworks shows, held the last Saturday in July, features 20,000 pyrotechnic wonders. Head to Asakusa early in the day to score a good seat. Check events listings for other fireworks displays around town.

August

This is the height of Japan's sticky, hot summer; school holidays mean sights may be crowded.

Asagaya Tanabata

Asagaya holds a Tanabata festival over the first weekend of August, with colorful lanterns strung up in its shōtengai (shopping arcade), Pearl Centre.

O-Bon

Three days in mid-August are set aside to honor the dead, when their spirits are said to return to the earth. Graves are swept, offerings are made and bon-odori (folk dances) take place. Many Tokyo residents return to their home towns; some shops may close too.

Lantern Floating

Toro nagashi is a photogenic summer tradition, connected to O-Bon, where candle-lit paper lanterns are floated down rivers. It takes place from mid-July to mid-August; two big ones happen at Chidori-ga-fuchi, along the Imperial Palace moat, and at Sumida-kōen in Asakusa.

Fukagawa Hachiman Matsuri

During this spirited festival at Tomioka Hachiman-gū, spectators throw water over the mikoshi carriers along the route. It's held in a big way only every three years; next up in 2020.

Asakusa Samba Carnival

On the last Saturday in August, Tokyo's Nikkei Brazilian community and local samba clubs turn Kaminarimon-dōri into one big party for the Asakusa Samba Carnival.

Kōenji Awa Odori

Kōenji Awa Odori is Tokyo's biggest awa odori (dance festival for O-Bon) with 12,000 participants in traditional costumes dancing their way through the streets over the last weekend of August.

September

Days are still warm, hot even – though the odd typhoon rolls through this time of year.

Moon Viewing

Full moons in September and October call for tsukimi, moon-viewing gatherings. People eat tsukimi dango – mochi (pounded rice) dumplings round like the moon.

Tokyo Game Show

Get your geek on when the Computer Entertainment Suppliers Association hosts Tokyo Game Show, a massive expo at Makuhari Messe in late September.

October

Pleasantly warm days and cool evenings make this an excellent time to be in Tokyo.

Design Touch

Tokyo Designers Week attracts the international design world with a large exhibition at Meiji-jingū Gaien, between late October and early November; shops and galleries around Aoyama and Gaienmae put on special displays.

Tokyo International Film Festival

During the last week in October, the Tokyo International Film Festival screens works from Japanese and international directors, with English subtitles.

Chrysanthemum Shows

Chrysanthemums are the flower of the season (and the royal family), and dazzling displays are put on from late October to mid-November in Hibiya-kōen and at shrines including Meiji-jingū and Yasukuni-jinja.

Halloween

Tokyo has gone mad for Halloween with thousands of costumed revelers converging on Shibuya Crossing. Shinjuku Ni-chōme and Roppongi see action, too.

Tokyo Grand Tea Ceremony

Held in late September or early October, at Hama-rikyū Onshi-teien and Edo-Tokyo Open Air Architecture Museum, this is a big outdoor tea party (http://tokyo-grand-tea-ceremony.jp/eng/index.html), with traditional tea ceremonies held in various styles, usually including one with English translation.

November

Tori-no-ichi

On 'rooster' days in November, 'O-tori' shrines such as Hanazono-jinja hold fairs called Tori-no-ichi (tori means 'rooster'); the day is set according to the old calendar, which marks days by the zodiac. Vendors hawk kumade – rakes that literally symbolize 'raking in the wealth'.

Shichi-go-san

This adorable festival in mid-November sees parents dress girls aged seven (shichi) and three (san) and boys aged five (go) in wee kimonos and head to Shintō shrines for blessings.

Kagurazaka Street Stage Ōedo Tour

Traditional music and story-telling in the streets of atmospheric Kagurazaka (http://kaguramachi.jp/en) and its shrine, Akagi-jinja; there's even a cameo appearance by the neighborhood's geisha.

Tokyo Filmex

Tokyo Filmex, which kicks off in late November, focuses on emerging directors in Asia and screens many films with English subtitles.

Autumn Leaves

The city's trees undergo magnificent seasonal transformations during kōyō (autumn foliage season); Rikugi-en and Koishikawa Kōrakuen have spectacular displays.

December

Restaurants and bars are filled with Tokyoites hosting bōnenkai (end-of-the-year parties). Commercial strips are decorated with seasonal illuminations.

International Robot Exhibition

The world's largest robot expo (www.nikkan.co.jp/eve/irex/english) takes place every other year at Tokyo Big Sight; next up in 2019.

Ako Gishi-sai

On 14 December, Sengaku-ji hosts a memorial service honoring the 47 rōnin (master less samurai) who famously avenged their fallen master; locals dressed as the loyal retainer's parade through nearby streets.

Winter Illuminations

Round two for Design Festa takes place in early November.

Toshikoshi Soba

Eating buckwheat noodles on New Year's Eve, a tradition called toshikoshi soba, is said to bring luck and longevity – the latter symbolized by the length of the noodles.

Joya-no-kane

Temple bells around Japan ring 108 times at midnight on 31 December, a purifying ritual called joya-no-kane. Sensō-ji draws the biggest crowds in Tokyo.

Money and costs in Tokyo

Daily costs

Budget: less than ¥8000

Dorm bed: ¥3000

Free sights such as temples and markets

Bowl of noodles: ¥750

Happy-hour drink: ¥500

24-hour subway pass: ¥600

Midrange: ¥8000–20,000

Double room at a business hotel: ¥14,000

Museum entry: ¥1000

Dinner for two at an izakaya (Japanese pub-eatery): ¥6000

Live music show: ¥3000

Top End: more than ¥20,000

Double room in a four-star hotel: ¥35,000

Sushi-tasting menu: ¥15,000

Box seat for kabuki: ¥21,000

Taxi ride back to the hotel: ¥3000

Bargaining

Bargaining is not common practice in Japan; flea markets are an exception.

Money

Post offices and most convenience stores have international ATMs. Credit cards are accepted at major establishments, though it's best to keep cash on hand.

ATMs

Most Japanese bank ATMs do not accept foreign-issued cards. Even if they display Visa and MasterCard logos, most accept only Japan-issued versions of these cards.

The following have ATMs that routinely work with most cards (including Visa, MasterCard, American Express, Plus, Cirrus and Maestro; some MasterCard and Maestro with IC chips may not work). Be aware that many banks place a limit on the amount of cash you can withdraw in one day (often around US$300).

7-Eleven (セブン・イレブン; www.sevenbank.co.jp/english) The Seven Bank ATMs at 7-Eleven convenience stores have English instructions and are available 24 hours a day. Considering that 7-Eleven convenience stores are ubiquitous, this is the easiest option for getting quick cash. Withdrawal limit of ¥100,000 per transaction.

Japan Post Bank (ゆうちょ銀行; www.jp-bank.japanpost.jp/en/ias/en_ias_index.html) Post offices have Japan Post Bank ATMs with English instructions; opening hours vary depending on the size of the post office, but are usually longer than regular post-office hours. Withdrawal limit of ¥50,000 per transaction.

Cash

More and more places in Tokyo accept credit cards but it's still a good idea to always keep at least several thousand yen on hand for local transport, inexpensive restaurants and shops (and even some moderately Priced restaurants and shops).

The currency in Japan is the yen (¥), and banknotes and coins are easily distinguishable. There are ¥1, ¥5, ¥10, ¥50, ¥100 and ¥500 coins; and ¥1000, ¥2000, ¥5000 and ¥10,000 banknotes (the ¥2000 note is very rarely seen). The ¥1 coin is a lightweight aluminum coin; the bronze-coloured ¥5 and silver-coloured ¥50 coins both have a hole punched in the middle. Prices may be listed using the kanji for yen (円). Prices are usually in Arabic numerals, but occasionally they are in traditional kanji.

Changing money

With a passport, you can change cash or travelers cheques at any Authorized Foreign Exchange Bank (signs are displayed in English), major post offices, some large hotels and most big department stores.

For currency other than US dollars, larger banks such as Sumitomo Mitsui (SMBC) and Tokyo-Mitsubishi UFJ (MUFG) are a better bet. They can usually change at least US, Canadian and Australian dollars, pounds sterling, euros and Swiss francs. Branches of these banks can be found near all major train stations.

MUFG also operates World Currency Shop (www.tokyo-card.co.jp/wcs/wcs-shop-e.php) foreign-exchange counters near major shopping centers. They will exchange a broader range of currencies, including Chinese yuan, Korean won and Taiwan, Hong Kong, Singapore and New Zealand dollars.

Note that you receive a better exchange rate when withdrawing cash from ATMs than when exchanging cash or travelers cheques in Tokyo.

Credit cards

Businesses that do take credit cards will often display the logo for the cards they accept. Visa is the most widely accepted, followed by MasterCard, American Express and Diners Club. Foreign-issued cards should work fine.

Tipping

It is not customary to tip, even in the most expensive restaurants and bars.

In high-end restaurants and hotels, a 10% service fee is usually added to the bill.

Planning tips

Advance planning

Three months before Purchase tickets for the Ghibli Museum; book a table at your top splurge restaurant.

One month before book any tickets for sumo, kabuki and Giants games online, and a spot on the Imperial Palace tour; scan web listings for festivals, events and exhibitions.

As soon as you arrive Look for free copies of Time Out Tokyo and Metropolis magazines at airports and hotels.

Resources

Go Tokyo (www.gotokyo.org) The city's official website includes information on sights, events and suggested itineraries.

Lonely Planet (www.lonelyplanet.com/tokyo) Destination information, hotel bookings, traveler forum and more.

Time Out Tokyo (www.timeout.jp) Arts and entertainment listings.

Tokyo Food Page (www.bento.com) City-wide restaurant coverage.

Tokyo Cheapo (https://tokyocheapo.com) Hints on how to do Tokyo on the cheap.

Top tips

Pick just a couple of proximate neighborhoods to explore in a day. Tokyo is huge and while public transport is effortlessly smooth, you don't want to spend half the day on it.

Splurge at lunch. Many restaurants – including those in notoriously Pricey districts like Ginza – offer midday meals that cost half (or less!) of what you'd find at dinner, and often for a meal that is not significantly smaller or lower in quality.

Rent a pocket Wi-Fi device. Tokyo has free Wi-Fi in spots but it's frustratingly clunky. Having constant internet access means you can use navigation apps to help you get around (as Tokyo's address system is famously confusing).

Walk. The further away you get from the subway stations (where rent is highest), the more independent local shops and restaurants you'll discover.

What to take

Tokyo hotels can be tiny, so bring as small a suitcase as possible.

You may be taking your shoes on and off a lot, so it helps to have ones that don't need lacing up.

What to wear

Casual clothes are fine, but you'll feel out of place if you're dressed as if you're heading to the gym. Tokyoites themselves are notoriously fashion conscious, though generally forgiving towards foreign tourists. Some high-end restaurants and bars do have a dress code, but this usually just means no sleeveless shirts or sandals on men.

Pre-departure checklist

Purchase a Japan Rail pass if you plan to travel extensively around the country.

Get an international licence if you'd like to drive a car (or a go-kart) in Tokyo.

Let your debit-/credit-card company know that you're heading away.

Reserve tickets for the Ghibli Museum or a sumo tournament, if you plan to visit either.

A foodie's day in Tokyo

So you came to Tokyo to eat? You'd need a whole month just to make it through the highlights of this world-class – some would say world's best – food city. But you can do a lot in a day, from trawling the markets and department stores to splurging on sushi and sake.

The best thing about Tokyo for food-lovers is you can eat and drink well on any budget. This itinerary hits the higher end of midrange (you could spend less, but you could spend a whole lot more). Take it down a notch by swapping one of the meals for ramen, which hardly ever disappoints.

Morning at the market

A foodie's day in Tokyo naturally begins with a morning trip to Tsukiji Market. The city's famed fish market is divided into two parts: the inner market (officially known as the Seafood Intermediate Wholesalers' Area) is where the tuna auction takes place most mornings around 6am – though you'll need to get there a lot earlier to join the queue if you want to score one of the 120 coveted spots to view the auction.

Not keen to rise so early? The outer market is where to go to find dozens of vendors selling essentials of Japanese cooking, such as the floss-like katsuo-bushi (flakes of dried bonito) used to make dashi (fish stock), the delicate sheets of nori (laver) used to wrap sushi rolls, and the tart, colorful pickles that complete the meal.

Scour the narrow lanes for takeaway counters such as Yamachō, which specializes in tamago-yaki, the rolled omelets served at sushi restaurants (but also good for breakfast). It can get very crowded here, so it does pay to come earlier rather than later. Fortunately, Turret Coffee, nearby maker of excellent lattes, opens on weekdays from 7am.

Note that Tsukiji inner market is scheduled to move to a new facility in Toyosu in October 2018. It's as yet unclear what visitor access will be like at the new market, so if the tuna auction has been on your bucket list the time to go is now!

Sushi lunch

A morning at the fish market is bound to work up an appetite for sushi. Dining at one of Tokyo's top-rated sushi counters is an experience of a lifetime, but it doesn't come cheap – which is why I love sushi for lunch. A meal at midday can cost half of what it does after dark (or even less, especially if you're not knocking back the sake).

You can't go wrong with Kyūbey, a Tokyo institution for over 80 years. Kyūbey offers a winning combination of reliable quality, welcoming service and cost performance. Go for the omakase (chef's choice), which features a selection of the day's best catch, prepared one piece at a time. Book ahead for the 11.30am seating (otherwise you'll have to queue).

I also love Kizushi for its Old-Tokyo vibe and Old-Tokyo taste: the sushi here is salted and marinated using techniques handed down through the generations. Also, the shop is in a charming wooden house. Reservations are recommended (and required for dinner).

Gourmet shopping in Ginza and Nihombashi

Ginza is Tokyo's premier shopping district and a gourmet hot spot. Classic department store Mitsukoshi has an excellent depachika (basement food hall), which carries perfectly ripe produce, sun-shaded tea, marbled wagyū (Japanese beef), sculptural sweets – you name it – from top producers. This is also where you'll find examples of Japan's famously unblemished (and super Pricey) fruit, given as gifts. Swank mall Ginza Six has a fittingly swank food hall as well. Boutique Akomeya sells artisanal ingredients, like soy sauce and miso, and beautiful traditional kitchen implements, such as shamoji (rice paddles) carved from hinoki (cedar) wood.

Neighbouring Nihombashi – home of the original fish market, before it set up in Tsukiji – has several, venerable old gourmet stores. Hit up the Coredo Muromachi complex, which has branches of Nihombashi native shops as well as famous purveyors from around Japan. See demonstrations of gorgeous, seasonal wagashi (Japanese sweets) being made at Tsuruya Yoshinobu.

Tea break

For years, Tokyo has been enamored with coffee, but recently the city is on a tea kick. There is a growing number of tea salons that can help you sort out your gyokuro (premium-grade green tea made from young leaves grown in the shade) from your sencha (green tea from unshaded young leaves) – not to mention all the other varieties of tea from various regions of Japan.

Sakurai Japanese Tea Experience may sound like a tourist trap but I assure you it is not. It's a gorgeous little space, with a minimalist counter, elegant tableware and a well-edited selection of teas served individually or as part of a tasting flight. They also do tea cocktails (the owner used to be a bartender).

On the more traditional side of things, there's Chashitsu Kaboku, run by Kyoto's most famous tea purveyor, 300-year-old Ippōdō. Here you can sample koicha, 'thick tea' served in formal tea ceremonies (much thicker than ordinary matcha, powdered green tea). Both shops sell packages of tea and tea utensils to take home.

Izakaya dinner

Just as you wouldn't visit the UK without eating in a pub, you can't visit Japan without eating at an izakaya. These are classic eating and drinking establishments, where sake (or beer, or whatever your drink of choice may be) is paired with small dishes of raw seafood, simmered tofu, fried chicken, braised pork... getting hungry again yet?

Shinsuke, near Ueno Station, is held up by many to be an ideal izakaya. It's been around for nearly 100 years, the menu is always seasonal (and the food never stodgy), the daiginjō (top-grade sake) always goes down smooth, and it always has a lively atmosphere. For something with a more contemporary edge, try cult favorite Narukiyo, in Shibuya, where you can tuck into decadent sashimi platters while listening to The Pogues and trying not to giggle at the cheeky decor.

Night cap

Wind down the day by raising a glass in Shinjuku, center of rainbow-coloured electrified streetscapes and a 24-hour entertainment scene. Zoetrope is one of the neighborhood's myriad tiny, laser-focused bars – with the world's best collection of Japanese whisky. BenFiddich is hands-down Tokyo's coolest cocktail bar, serving up strong, herbal concoctions in dreamy surrounds.

Touring Tokyo on the Yamanote line

Tokyoites often say that the best way to get to know their city is to travel station by station around the Yamanote line, the city's iconic elevated loop line, running since 1925. The route includes well-known neighborhoods like Shinjuku, Ueno, Akihabara and Shibuya, but also local spots that few outsiders visit.

Examined up close, Tokyo is dramatically different north to south, east to west and even from station to station. Make the rounds of all 29 stations on the Yamanote line and Tokyo appears less like a cohesive city than a collection of self-contained towns. A complete loop takes roughly an hour; work in a handful of stops, and it's a perfect one-day introduction to the city.

Komagome, Nishi-Nippori and Ueno

Start at Komagome, due north. Few people travel to this sleepy 'hood, even though it is home to the city's prettiest garden, Rikugi-en. Here, follow the path through wooded groves and over bridges to the teahouse, which overlooks the garden's pond, for a cup of matcha (powdered green tea). I can't think of a better way to begin the day.

Two stops – on a soto-mawari (clockwise) train – takes you to Nishi-Nippori, where the highlight is Yanaka Ginza. This is one of the city's best examples of a classic shōtengai (market street).

The northeast section of the city, and this area in particular, has seen less development than many other parts of Tokyo. Tokyoites love this nostalgic mid-20th century atmosphere, marked by narrow alleys, low-slung buildings and vintage signs.

Ueno, two stops further, is the major hub of northeast Tokyo and also the city's old cultural heart. It's here that you'll find the Tokyo National Museum, which houses the world's best collection of Japanese art. The museum and several more (plus centuries-old shrines and temples) are located inside the sprawling park Ueno-kōen. There are a number of excellent, historic restaurants in this part of town, too. Beautiful Innsyoutei, in an old wooden building inside the park, is a great choice for lunch.

Akihabara, Tokyo Station and Yūrakuchō

From Ueno, as the train wends southward along the city's eastern edge, the buildings become bigger and taller and the urban bustle more palpable. Akihabara – affectionately known as 'Akiba' – is synonymous with Japanese pop culture. Fans of anime, manga, gaming and idol singers, along with tech geeks, robot enthusiasts and gadget collectors, gather here to bask in the glow of the LED-lit shop fronts and to scour shops like Mandarake Complex and Yodobashi Akiba for new goods to feed their passions.

Also in Akihabara is the old Manseibashi Station, built in 1912. It served as the eastern terminus for the Chūō line – the east–west route that pierces the center of the Yamanote line – until it was retired in the 1940s. The station building, recently restored, now hosts the upscale shopping and dining center, mAAch ecute.

Tokyo Station, in Marunouchi, is the city's central station and the terminus for the nation's network of shinkansen (bullet train) lines. The brick structure, modelled after the great stations of Europe, was built in 1914 and restored in 2014. The surrounding neighborhood, Marunouchi, is at the center of establishment Tokyo, where many of the country's biggest companies have their headquarters, and just a stone's throw from the Imperial Palace.

The next two stops, Yūrakuchō and Shimbashi, represent the beating heart of 'salaryman culture' – that of the hardworking, hard-drinking, grey-suited company employee. Their haunts include smoky yakitori (grilled chicken skewers) stands crammed under and along the rail lines. Stop by Manpuku Shokudō, one such place under the Yamanote line tracks in Yūrakuchō, for happy-hour drinks (it's open all day).

Hamamatsu-chō to Ebisu

The southern stretch of the line, where it skirts near Tokyo Bay, is corporate central, full of glistening high-rises (where there were once tidal flats). Shinagawa, a shinkansen station, and Ōsaki, the southernmost node on the loop, are two big transit hubs. Past Ōsaki, the train enters the wealthy southwest quarter of the city. Before the city began to take its modern form, roughly 100 to 150 years ago, this area was largely rice and tea fields, villages and country villas.

Today these neighborhoods, such as Meguro and Ebisu, are known for genteel residential pockets and fashionable shopping and dining scenes.

Ebisu is the town that beer built: the original Yebisu beer factory went up here in the late 19th century and operated until 1988. The old, red-brick structure now holds the Beer Museum Yebisu. It's adjacent to the open-air culture and shopping complex Ebisu Garden Place, where you'll also find Tokyo's photography museum, TOP Museum. Ebisu is a great place to grab a bite. Check out favorite local hangout, Ebisu-yokochō – a hip imagining of a Yūrakuchō-style food alley – or queue for ramen at trendy Afuri.

Shibuya, Shinjuku and Ikebukuro

Northwest Tokyo is synonymous with the city's boom years in the second half of the 20th century. This is especially true of the hubs Shibuya, Shinjuku and Ikebukuro, which more than any other districts feel like cities unto themselves. This is the Tokyo of giant video screens, concrete towers, blazing LED nightscapes, serious pedestrian traffic and a 24-hour vibe.

Right outside Shibuya Station is Shibuya Crossing, Tokyo's mesmerizing (and quite likely the country's busiest) intersection. Beyond the station is the neighborhood's pedestrianized main strip, Shibuya Center-gai, which is lined with clothing shops, fast-food restaurants and a blinding array of glowing signs. Shibuya is full of tempting bars, nightclubs, karaoke parlors and live music halls. Just save some energy for...

Shinjuku. This is the city at its most bombastic, bustling and overwhelming. Shinjuku's train station is Japan's busiest, with some 3 million people passing through every day. The city capital is here, in the impressive (or imposing, depending on your taste) Tokyo Metropolitan Government Building complex. Atop Building 1, at 202m, there's a free observatory, with panoramic views over the glittering city – you can see how massive Tokyo really is. Last entry is 10.30pm.

Shinjuku has nightlife in spades. Go broke at the sky-high New York Bar in the Park Hyatt or go bar-hopping among the boho wooden shacks of Golden Gai. (If you're not staying nearby, keep in mind that the last trains leave Shinjuku around 12.30am.)

You can complete the loop, heading through Ikebukuro – another giant hub for commuter trains, with more department stores, restaurants and bars galore. Or maybe give it a go tomorrow morning, when the trains start running again at 4.45am.

Yamanote Line travel tips

Most Yamanote trains make a continuous loop but some may terminate at Ikebukuro or Osaki, meaning you have to get off the train and wait for the next one.

Between 7am and midnight trains run every 3 to 5 minutes; less frequently in the early-morning hours.

Trains are jam-packed during the morning rush (7am to 9.30am); the evening rush (around 5pm to 8pm) is not quite as bad as the morning commute.

A one-day Tokyo Combination Ticket (adult/child ¥1590/800) covers all central Tokyo JR lines (including the Yamanote) plus city subways and buses. These tickets can be purchased at any midori-no-madoguchi ticket counter in major JR stations (such as Shinjuku, Tokyo and Ueno).

The Yamanote line is part of the JR (Japan Rail) network so is covered by the JR pass.

Without a pass, ticket fares are calculated by distance, with short trips costing ¥140 and the longest one (a full half-loop) costing ¥260.

Tokyo in spring: best things to see and do

Like everywhere in Japan, spring in Tokyo means sakura (cherry) blossoms. This is an obvious reason to visit, but by no means the only one. There are also traditional festivals, sumo, seasonal delicacies and a whole lot more in bloom in the city's parks and gardens.

Bear in mind that spring is the most popular time of year to visit Japan and book your accommodation well in advance. Be especially wary of the string of national holidays, known as Golden Week; it's a peak travel period for Japanese that can drive up hotel rates. In 2018, Golden Week will run from 28 April to 6 May.

See the cherry blossoms, of course!

Like someone took a paintbrush to the city, large swathes of Tokyo go from grey to blush pink come cherry-blossom season. Parks like Yoyogi-kōen and Ueno-kōen are famous for sake-drenched cherry-blossom-viewing parties called hanami. Waterside promenades, such as the one alongside Naka-Meguro's canal, Meguro-gawa, and the one opposite the Imperial Palace's moat, Chidori-ga-fuchi, erupt with canopies of blossoms.

Sakura (cherry) season, which begins in late March or early April is like Carnival – one collective, citywide excuse to let go of daily cares and live for the moment. It's a centuries-old tradition, inspired by the fleeting beauty of the blossoms, which last no longer than two weeks. What does last longer is all the sakura-themed treats sold at convenience stores and chain cafes. Sakura latte, anyone?

And see other blooms as well

Cherry blossoms hog the spotlight, but spring sees a whole cavalcade of seasonal blooms. They may not be an excuse to have a drinking party in the afternoon, but they definitely draw plenty of admirers. Bonus: from mid-April until early June (when the rainy season sets in) the weather is warmer and sunnier than it is during sakura season.

Soon after the last cherry blossoms fall, bold, bright azalea (tsutsuji) flowers begin appearing around the city. (Unless you visit during this season, from the second week of April through the first week of May, you may not realize just how much of Tokyo's ornamental shrubbery is made up of azaleas.) The most dramatic spot to see them is at shrine Nezu-jinja, which has a whole garden of them – some 3000 shrubs representing over a hundred varietals.

Following a week or so behind the azaleas are the languid, lavender blooms of the wisteria (fuji-no-hana). Kameido Tenjin, a large but otherwise somewhat ignored shrine in Tokyo's far eastern edge, is the best place to see them. There's a famous photo spot here (warning: it gets very crowded) where you can capture the shrine's signature red, arched bridges with the drooping flowers in the foreground. Koishikawa Kōrakuen – better known for its plum blossoms and fall foliage – also has a small area with some wisteria trellises.

In June – the not-quite-summer rainy season – come the irises, which were a favorite of the late 19th-century Empress Shoken. Her husband (the Emperor Meiji) planted an iris garden for her at what is now Meiji-jingū Gyoen, the pretty strolling garden attached to Meiji-jingū. There are some 1500 irises here, which I can be sure is a fairly accurate figure because (according to shrine's website) staff count the blossoms every day. The June rains also bring hydrangea (ajisai), which are a favorite of Tokyo urban gardeners. True fans of these magnificent, multi-hued orbs will want to make a pilgrimage to Meigetsu-in, a temple in seaside Kamakura (an hour south of Tokyo) that is also known as Ajisai-dera ('Hydrangea Temple').

You could also go wild and take an overnight ferry down to Hachijō-jima to see the freesias, which bloom at roughly the same time as Tokyo's sakura (and where it will definitely be warm and sunny).

Catch a traditional festival

May is the start of matsuri (festival) season, when shrines take their kami (gods) out for a spin on mikoshi, ornately decorated portable shrines that are paraded through the neighborhood. Tokyo's matsuri go back centuries – to the founding years of the city in the 1600s – and the mikoshi-bearers look the part. Expect to see plenty of colorful happi (short, cotton kimono-style jackets), hachimaki (bandanas tied as headbands) and, for the men, fundoshi (the loin clothes that you see on sumo wrestlers).

The Sanja Matsuri, put on by Asakusa-jinja, is the biggest matsuri of them all, known to draw over a million spectators. It's held on the third weekend in May (in 2018: 18 to 20 May), with the big parade happening on the Saturday. In June, Hie-jinja hosts the Sannō Matsuri, a similar (but smaller) spectacle that happens only on even-numbered years. The festival runs from 7 to 17 June and in 2018 the parade will take place on Friday 8 June.

Or a festival that's just a little bit naughty

Might I also suggest a detour to Kawasaki (just south of Tokyo) for the annual Kanamara Matsuri, otherwise known as the penis festival? Like other traditional festivals, this one sees a parade of locals hoisting mikoshi through the streets – except that many of these mikoshi are in fact strapped with giant phalluses. It's a jubilant affair, with some revelers arriving in drag or fancy dress. There are all sorts of naughty talismans and suggestive snacks available, too. Don't miss the locals carving radishes into, ahem, you know.

Kawasaki shrine Kanayama-jinja hosts the event, which takes place on the first Sunday of April (1 April in 2018). The shrine is known historically as a place to pray for a happy marriage and a healthy pregnancy but also for protection from sexually transmitted diseases.

See sumo wrestlers in the ring... and holding babies

The second of Tokyo's three annual grand sumo tournaments takes place in mid-May (from 13 May to 27 May in 2018) at the national sumo stadium, Ryōgoku Kokugikan. A few weeks earlier, on 29 April, Sensō-ji hosts its annual Naki-zumo event, which pairs sumo wrestlers and babies in a cry-off. The wrestlers pull faces, competing to make their baby cry the loudest. This may sound bizarre (and a little mean) but the Japanese have an age-old belief that a crying baby will grow up to be big and healthy. Sometimes the babies are dressed up as tiny sumo wrestlers.

Taste spring specialties

Japanese food is famous for being exceptionally seasonal and while nowadays, and especially in Tokyo, you can get just about anything year-round, you do pay quite a bit for it. So for a populace that has spent the last few months eating an awful lot of cabbage, daikon and mikan (satsuma mandarin oranges), the bounty of spring is a real boon. The first sign of the changing season is the appearance on menus of takenoko (bamboo shoots). The tender, slightly bitter shoots are usually parboiled or steamed with rice (a dish called takikomi gohan). There are also sansai, a catch-all term (meaning 'mountain vegetables') for the various roots and shoots – such as fukinoto (butterbur buds) and warabi (fiddlehead fern) – that can be foraged in the mountains in spring. They are especially delicious served as tempura.

Asparagus, spring onions, nanohana (rapeseed) and mizuna (a kind of young mustard green) appear this time of year in supermarkets and farmers' markets, like Farmer's Market @UNU. And finally, in June, the sakura bear fruit. (Not Tokyo's ornamental ones, sadly, but ones in orchards to the north.) Check department store basement food halls, like Food Show, for satonishiki, Japan's most prized variety of cherry. They're small, more vermilion – like the color of a shrine's torii gate – than deep red, with a rich sheen and a sweet-meets-tart flavor.

Best places to see cherry blossoms in Japan

Springtime in Japan and the country watches and waits for the first sakura (cherry) trees to burst into bloom. Once they do, people flock to parks and squares for hanami (cherry-blossom viewing). The romance is passionate but fleeting, lasting only a week or two.

Starting from Kyūshū in the south sometime in March, regular blossom forecasts keep the public updated as the sakura zensen (cherry-tree blossom line) advances northward, usually passing through the Kansai and Kantō regions of Honshū in early April. Latecomers can catch the blossoms in late April and sometimes early May in Tōhoku, the northernmost region of Honshū. Here are just five of the top spots across Japan to join the hanami party.

Yoshino, Kansai

Yoshino is Japan's most famous cherry-blossom destination, and for a few weeks in early to mid-April, the blossoms of thousands of cherry trees form a floral carpet gradually ascending the mountainsides. It's definitely a sight worth seeing – and one that many Japanese long to see once in their life – but this does mean that the narrow streets of the village become jammed tight with thousands of visitors. You'll have to be content with a day trip (doable from Nara, or even Osaka) unless you've booked accommodation long in advance. Once the cherry-blossom petals fall, the crowds depart and Yoshino reverts back to a quiet village with a handful of shrines and temples.

Maruyama-kōen, Kyoto

This one is a tough call – Kyoto has so many fantastic places to see the blossoms. But it's safe to say that the most iconic hanami spot in the city is Maruyama-kōen (Maruyama Park). In the middle of the park is the Gion Shidare-zakura, the 'Weeping Cherry of Gion', named for its proximity to famed entertainment district, Gion, where geiko (Kyoto's geisha) still perform. The over-10m-tall tree, whose blossom-fringed branches arch gracefully almost to the ground, is illuminated in the evening, from dusk until midnight. Oh, and there are some 680 other cherry trees in the park so you can bet on lots of picnics taking place here. Come early to grab a good spot. And later on, take a stroll along the nearby canal, the Gion Shirakawa, lined with cherry trees and also lit up at night.

Yoyogi-kōen, Tokyo

Like Kyoto, Tokyo has many popular cherry blossom spots. While it's not the most historic – that would be Ueno-kōen – or the most picturesque – that would be Shinjuku-gyoen – I 're doubling down on Yoyogi-kōen (Yoyogi Park) because it is just the most fun. It's a huge, sprawling park with tufty grass and plenty of cherry trees, with room for everyone and yet it still becomes a sea of people growing more and more unsteady as the day gives way to night. I 've seen barbecues here, turntables and portable karaoke machines, more selfie sticks than I care to count and the odd guy in nothing but his shorts. The only thing Yoyogi-kōen is short on is public toilets (prepare to queue).

Arakurayama Sengen-kōen, Fuji Five Lakes

The view from the Chureitō Pagoda here is the ultimate sakura money shot: in one frame you get a classic five-story pagoda, with curving eaves and vermillion accents, a frothy sea of cherry blossoms beneath it, and on the horizon, triumphant Mt Fuji still draped in snow. (Odds are you've seen the image on a guidebook cover or two.) So what if the pagoda itself isn't actually old (it's a war memorial from the 1960s) and you have to climb 397 steps to get here? Arakurayama Sengen-kōen (a park home to a not-so-shabby 680 sakura trees) is in Fuji-Yoshida, a city at the base of Mt Fuji. It's just about possible as a day trip from Tokyo, but you could also budget an extra day or two for hiking in the foothills of the Fuji Five Lakes region, for the chance of even more Mt Fuji views.

Hirosaki-kōen, Tōhoku (Northern Honshū)

Hirosaki-kōen (Hirosaki Park) is a huge green space (nearly 50 hectares!) covering the grounds of what used to be the castle Hirosaki-jō. All that remains of the actual castle is a 200-year-old keep, but the park is marbled with the old moats, which are now flanked by sakura and crisscrossed with photogenic arching bridges. There are over 2500 cherry trees here and given that Hirosaki, way up north in Aomori Prefecture, is not the population center that Tokyo (or even Kyoto) is, you can expect a bit more room to move around. Bonus: you can rent peddle boats to take out on the moats, which are invariably covered in pink petals.

For more

There are countless other parks, gardens and picturesque waterways across the country where you can gaze upon the pretty blooms. Monitor the cherry-blossom forecast for each region and see the latest reports at kyuhoshi.com/japan-cherry-blossom-forecast.

Tokyo in winter: what to see, do and eat

Tokyo's winter charms are one of the city's best-kept secrets. This means that as well as a festive atmosphere and crisp, clear days perfect for soaking in hot springs and spotting Mt Fuji, visitors get to enjoy all the city has to offer with far fewer crowds.

Just keep in mind that many attractions close some or all of the first week of January, for the New Year holiday.

Visit a shrine on New Year's Day

Tokyoites may not be a pious bunch but nearly everyone turns up for hatsumode, the ritual first shrine visit of the New Year. The most popular spot is far and away Meiji-jingū – which gets literally millions of visitors over the first few days of January (expect long lines!) – but any of Tokyo's larger shrines attract visitors shortly after midnight. It's tradition to buy new omamori (charms) and omikuji (fortunes written on strips of paper) and to turn in your old ones, which will be ritually burned.

See Mt Fuji

Winter is the best time of year for spotting Mt Fuji on the horizon. Draped in snow, the volcano's cone is also extra picturesque this time of year. Top viewing spots in the city include the observatories at Tokyo Metropolitan Government Building, Tokyo Tower, Tokyo Sky Tree and Roppongi Hills' Tokyo City View. Even better: make the brisk climb to the summit of Takao-san, on the western edge of Tokyo, or a trip down to the lake, Ashi-no-ko, in Hakone for spectacular views of Japan's iconic peak.

Toss beans for luck

Setsubun, a centuries-old observance, takes place every year on 3 February (the day before the first day of spring on the old lunar calendar). It's a sort of spring-cleaning of the spiritual kind: people gather at shrines and temples to toss toasted soybeans while shouting, 'Oni wa soto! Fuku wa uchi!' ('Devils out! Luck in!'). Then, to double down on luck, it is customary to eat one's age in soybeans. Tokyo neighborhood Shimo-Kitazawa takes the festivities up a notch with its Tengū Matsuri. In addition to the requisite bean throwing, there is a parade of locals carrying the giant, red head of a tengū – a long-nosed demon, who is equal parts protective deity and fearsome troublemaker. In 2018 the festival runs from 27 to 29 January, with the parade on 28 January.

Soak in hot springs

The winter chill is just one more reason to seek out an onsen (hot spring) bath. Make a day out of it at one of the city's spa complexes. These include Ōedo Onsen Monogatari, which bills itself as an onsen amusement park, and Spa LaQua, which has over a dozen baths and saunas from which to choose. You can also go ultra-local by taking a dip in a sentō, a community bathhouse. Some favorites include Rokuryū Kōsen, Jakotsu-yu and Komparu-yu. (Note that spas usually deny entry to guests with tattoos, but sentō usually have an open policy; the policy will typically be posted on the front door.)

Stroll under the plum blossoms

The first sign of spring in Japan isn't sakura (cherry) blossoms; it's ume (plum) blossoms, which appear in the capital in late February. Like sakura, the photogenic flowers come in myriad shades of pink (though they're a little bigger and hardier). And while ume don't draw the party crowds that sakura does, they do occasion a visit to one of the sites that is famous for them, such as Koishikawa Kōrakuen or Yushima Tenjin.

Admire the Christmas lights

Christmas in Japan is a largely secular holiday and one of the most important date nights of the year. (Think of Christmas and New Year as being opposite what they are in the west; here New Year is for families and Christmas is for couples.) Tokyo's commercial districts go all out with illuminations that last the whole month of December. One particularly magical spot is Keyaki-zaka on the edge of Roppongi Hills.

Catch the big boys in action

The first grand sumo tournament of the year kicks off at Tokyo's Ryōgoku Kokugikan in January. The tournament lasts two weeks, with matches going on all morning and afternoon each day; the most coveted tickets are for the last days of the tournament (when the stakes are highest), so book those early. The tournament runs from 14 to 28 January in 2018 (tickets on sale from 26 December 2017).

Warm up with winter dishes

The classic dish of winter is nabe, which is any possible combination of meat, seafood, vegetables and tofu simmered in broth in a big earthen pot set on the table. It's invariably a social dish, as one pot serves several. Lots of izakaya (Japanese-style pubs) have it on the menu in winter. Try chanko nabe – the protein-rich stew on which sumo wrestlers feast in order to gain weight and strength – at Kappō Yoshiba.

Hit the slopes near Tokyo

Tokyo's closest ski and snowboarding spot is Gala Yuzawa, just a 75-minute ride away on the shinkansen (bullet train). The train literally deposits you at the resort: the gondola leaves from the same station. Full gear rental (including snow attire) is available, meaning you can show up empty-handed. Gala Yuzawa gets consistently good snow (the adjacent hot spring town, Echigo-Yuzawa Onsen was, after all, the setting for Kawabata Yasunari's novel Snow Country). Take advantage of the JR Tokyo Wide train pass (adult/child ¥10,000/5000), which covers three consecutive days of return travel on the shinkansen to Gala Yuzawa, plus limited express trains to and from Nikkō, the Izu Peninsula and Narita Airport.

Grab a lucky bag

Just as shrines have hatsumode, shops have hatsuuri – the first sale of the year, which happens just after the New Year (and sometimes on New Year's Day). For this occasion, many shops (and especially department stores) prepare fukubukuro, or lucky bags, containing an unknown quantity of mystery merchandise at a steep discount. Devotees of a particular shop will queue for hours for a coveted fukubukuro; sold in limited quantities they often sell out on the first day.

Kyoto

Kyoto is old Japan writ large: atmospheric temples, sublime gardens, traditional teahouses and geisha scurrying to secret liaisons.

Japan's spiritual heart

This is a city of some 2000 temples and shrines: a city of true masterpieces of religious architecture, such as the retina-burning splendor of Kinkaku-ji (the famed Golden Pavilion) and the cavernous expanse of Higashi Hongan-ji. It's where robed monks shuffle between temple buildings, prayer chants resonate through stunning Zen gardens, and the faithful meditate on tatami-mat floors. Even as the modern city buzzes and shifts all around, a waft of burning incense, or the sight of a bright vermillion torii gate marking a shrine entrance, are regular reminders that Kyoto remains the spiritual heart of Japan.

A trip for the taste buds

Few cities of this size pack such a punch when it comes to their culinary cred, and at its heart is Nishiki Market ('Kyoto's kitchen'). Kyoto is crammed with everything from Michelin-starred restaurants, chic cocktail bars, cool cafes and sushi spots to food halls, izakaya (Japanese pub-eateries), craft-beer bars and old-school noodle joints. Splurge on the impossibly refined cuisine known as kaiseki while gazing over your private garden, taste the most delicate tempura in a traditional building, slurp down steaming bowls of ramen elbow-to-elbow with locals, then slip into a sugar coma from a towering matcha (powdered green tea) sundae.

A city of artisans

While the rest of Japan has adopted modernity with abandon, the old ways are still clinging on in Kyoto. With its roots as the cultural capital of the country, it's no surprise that many traditional arts and crafts are kept alive by artisans from generation to generation. Wander the streets downtown, through historic Gion and past machiya (traditional Japanese townhouses) in the Nishijin textile district to find ancient specialty shops from tofu sellers, washi (Japanese handmade paper) and tea merchants, to exquisite lacquerware, handcrafted copper chazutsu (tea canisters) and indigo-dyed noren (hanging curtains).

Cultural encounters

If you don't know your matcha (powdered green tea) from your manga (Japanese comic), have never slept on a futon or had a bath with naked strangers, then it doesn't matter as this is the place to immerse yourself in the intricacies of Japanese culture. Whether you watch matcha being whisked in a traditional tea ceremony, spend the night in a ryokan, get your gear off and soak in an onsen, join a raucous hanami (cherry-blossom viewing) party or discover the art of Japanese cooking – you'll come away one step closer to understanding the unique Japanese way of life.

Buddhist Temples in Kyoto

Kiyomizu-dera

Top choice Buddhist temple in Southern Higashiyama

Details:

1-294 Kiyomizu, Higashiyama-ku

075-551-1234

http://www.kiyomizudera.or.jp/

Hours: 6am-6pm, closing times vary seasonally

Price: adult/child ¥400/200

A buzzing hive of activity perched on a hill overlooking the basin of Kyoto, Kiyomizu-dera is one of Kyoto's most popular and most enjoyable temples. It may not be a tranquil refuge, but it represents the favored expression of faith in Japan. The excellent website is a great first port of call for information on the temple, plus a how-to guide to praying here. Note that the Main Hall is undergoing renovations and may be covered, though is still accessible.

This ancient temple was first built in 798, but the present buildings are reconstructions dating from 1633. As an affiliate of the Hossō school of Buddhism, which originated in Nara, it has successfully survived the many intrigues of local Kyoto schools of Buddhism through the centuries and is now one of the most famous landmarks of the city (for which reason it can get very crowded during spring and autumn).

The Hondō (Main Hall) has a huge verandah that is supported by pillars and juts out over the hillside. Just below this hall is the waterfall Otowa-no-taki, where visitors drink sacred waters believed to bestow health and longevity. Dotted around the precincts are other halls and shrines. At Jishu-jinja, the shrine up the steps above the main hall, visitors try to ensure success in love by closing their eyes and walking about 18m between a pair of stones – if you miss the stone, your desire for love won't be fulfilled! Note that you can ask someone to guide you, but if you do, you'll need someone's assistance to find your true love.

Before you enter the actual temple precincts, check out the Tainai-meguri, the entrance to which is just to the left (north) of the pagoda that is located in front of the main entrance to the temple (¥100 donation). I won't tell you too much about it as it will ruin the experience. Suffice to say that by entering the Tainai-meguri, you are symbolically entering the womb of a female bodhi-sattva. When you get to the rock in the darkness, spin it in either direction to make a wish.

The steep approach to the temple is known as Chawan-zaka (Teapot Lane) and is lined with shops selling Kyoto handicrafts, local snacks and souvenirs.

Check the website for the scheduling of special night-time illuminations of the temple held in spring and autumn.

Daitoku-ji

Top choice Buddhist temple in Imperial Palace & Around

Details:

53 Daitokuji-chō, Murasakino, Kita-ku

Hours: hours for subtemples vary

Price: admission to subtemples varies

For anyone with the slightest fondness for Japanese gardens, don't miss this network of lanes dotted with atmospheric Zen temples. Daitoku-ji is the main temple here and serves as headquarters for the Rinzai Daitoku-ji school of Zen Buddhism. It's not usually open to the public but there are several subtemples with superb carefully raked karen-sensui (dry-rock garden) well worth making the trip out to this part of the city. Highlights among the subtemples open to the public include Daisen-in, Kōtō-in (closed for renovations until 2019), Ryōgen-in and Zuihō-in.

Daitoku-ji is on the eastern side of the grounds. It was founded in 1319, burnt down in the next century and rebuilt in the 16th century. The San-mon gate (1589) has a self-carved statue of its erector, the famous tea master Sen no Rikyū, on its 2nd story.

The Karasuma subway line to Kitaōji Station is the fastest way to get here. From Kitaōji Station, walk west along Kitaōji-dōri for about 15 minutes. You'll see the temple complex on your right. The main entrance is a bit north of Kitaōji. If you enter from the main gate, which is on the east side of the complex, you'll soon find Daitoku-ji on your right. Alternatively, take bus 205 or 206 from Kyoto Station to the Daitokuji-mae bus stop.

Tōfuku-ji

Top choice Buddhist temple in Kyoto Station & South Kyoto

Details:

15-778 Honmahi, Higashiyama-ku

075-561-0087

Hours: 9am-4pm

Price: Hōjō garden ¥400, Tsūten-kyō bridge ¥400

Home to a spectacular garden, several superb structures and beautiful precincts, Tōfuku-ji is one of the best temples in Kyoto. It's well worth a visit and can easily be paired with a trip to Fushimi Inari-Taisha (the temples are linked by the Keihan and JR train lines). The present temple complex includes 24 subtemples. The huge San-mon is the oldest Zen main gate in Japan, the Hōjō (Abbot's Hall) was reconstructed in 1890, and the gardens were laid out in 1938.

The northern garden has stones and moss neatly arranged in a checkerboard pattern. From a viewing platform at the back of the gardens you can observe the Tsūten-kyō (Bridge to Heaven), which spans a valley filled with maples.

Founded in 1236 by the priest Enni, Tōfuku-ji belongs to the Rinzai sect of Zen Buddhism. As this temple was intended to compare with Tōdai-ji and Kōfuku-ji in Nara, it was given a name combining characters from the names of each of these temples.

Tōfuku-ji offers regular Zen meditation sessions for beginners, but don't expect coddling or English-language explanations: this is the real deal. Get a Japanese speaker to enquire at the temple about the next session (it holds about four a month for beginners).

Note that Tōfuku-ji is one of Kyoto's most famous autumn-foliage spots, and it is invariably packed during the peak of colors in November. Otherwise, it's often very quiet.

Saihō-ji

Top choice Buddhist temple in Arashiyama & Sagano

Details:

56 Jingatani-chō, Matsuo, Nishikyō-ku

Price: ¥3000

Saihō-ji, one of Kyoto's best-known gardens, is famed for its superb moss garden, hence the temple's nickname: Koke-dera (Moss Temple). The heart-shaped garden, laid out in 1339 by Musō Kokushi, surrounds a tranquil pond and is simply stunning. In order to limit the number of visitors, you must apply to visit at least one week in advance, though the earlier the better to avoid disappointment.

To make a reservation to visit, you need to send a postcard and include your name, number of visitors, occupation, age (you must be over 18 years) and desired date (choice of alternative dates preferred), along with a self-addressed postcard for a reply to your address (in Japan or overseas). The address to send it to is: Saihō-ji, 56 Kamigaya-chō, Matsuo, Nishikyō-ku, Kyoto-shi 615-8286, JAPAN. Your return postcard will let you know the date and time of your visit.

When you arrive at Saiho-ji, visitors are required to copy a sutra with an ink brush. Foreigners are generally just required to write their name, address and a prayer, rather than attempt to copy the sutra. Once in the garden, you are free to explore on your own and at your own pace. The whole visit usually takes around one hour.

While the process might seem a little over the top, it's certainly worth the small effort to organize, particularly if you have a fondness for Japanese gardens.

Chion-in

Top choice Buddhist temple in Southern Higashiyama

Details:

400 Rinka-chō, Higashiyama-ku

http://www.chion-in.or.jp/

Hours: 9am-4.30pm

Price: inner buildings & garden adult/child ¥500/250, grounds free

A collection of soaring buildings and spacious courtyards, Chion-in serves as the headquarters of the Jōdo sect, the largest school of Buddhism in Japan. It's the most popular pilgrimage temple in Kyoto and it's always a hive of activity. For visitors with a taste for the grand, this temple is sure to satisfy.

Chion-in was established in 1234 on the site where Hōnen, one of the most famous figures in Japanese Buddhism, taught his brand of Buddhism (Jōdo, or Pure Land, Buddhism) and eventually fasted to death.

The oldest of the present buildings date to the 17th century. The two-story San-mon temple gate is the largest in Japan. The immense Miei-dō Hall (Main Hall) contains an image of Hōnen. It's connected to another hall, the Dai Hōjō, by a 'nightingale' floor (that sings and squeaks at every move, making it difficult for intruders to move about quietly). Miei-dō Hall is currently under restoration and closed to the public. It's expected to be finished by 2020.

Up a flight of steps southeast of the main hall is the temple's giant bell, which was cast in 1633 and weighs 70 tons. It is the largest bell in Japan. The bell is rung by the temple's monks 108 times on New Year's Eve each year.

Eikan-dō

Top choice Buddhist temple in Northern Higashiyama

Details:

48 Eikandō-chō, Sakyō-ku

075-761-0007

http://www.eikando.or.jp/

Hours: 9am-5pm

Price: adult/child ¥600/400

Perhaps Kyoto's most famous (and most crowded) autumn-foliage destination, Eikan-dō is a superb temple just a short walk south of the famous Path of Philosophy. Eikan-dō is made interesting by its varied architecture, its gardens and its works of art. It was founded as Zenrin-ji in 855 by the priest Shinshō, but the name was changed to Eikan-dō in the 11th century to honor the philanthropic priest Eikan.

In the Amida-dō hall at the southern end of the complex is a famous statue of Mikaeri Amida Buddha glancing backwards.

From Amida-dō, head north to the end of the curving covered garyūrō (walkway). Change into the sandals provided, then climb the steep steps up the mountainside to the Tahō-tō pagoda, from where there's a fine view across the city.

For most of November, the admission fee increases to ¥1000 to visit during the day for the autumn leaves, and the temple stays open to 8.30pm for the autumn nighttime illumination (¥600).

Ginkaku-ji

Top choice Buddhist temple in Northern Higashiyama

Details:

2 Ginkaku-ji-chō, Sakyō-ku

Hours: 8.30am-5pm Mar-Nov, 9am-4.30pm Dec-Feb

Price: adult/child ¥500/300

Home to a sumptuous garden and elegant structures, Ginkaku-ji is one of Kyoto's premier sites. The temple started its life in 1482 as a retirement villa for Shogun Ashikaga Yoshimasa, who desired a place to retreat from the turmoil of a civil war. While the name Ginkaku-ji literally translates as 'Silver Pavilion', the shogun's ambition to cover the building with silver was never realized. After Yoshimasa's death, the villa was converted into a temple.

Walkways lead through the gardens, which include meticulously raked cones of white sand (said to be symbolic of a mountain and a lake), tall pines and a pond in front of the temple. A path also leads up the mountainside through the trees.

Note that Ginkaku-ji is one of the city's most popular sites, and it is almost always crowded, especially during spring and autumn. I strongly recommend visiting right after it opens or just before it closes.

Tenryū-ji

Top choice Buddhist temple in Arashiyama & Sagano

Details:

68 Susukinobaba-chō, Saga-Tenryū-ji, Ukyō-ku

075-881-1235

http://www.tenryuji.com/

Hours: 8.30am-5.30pm, to 5pm mid-Oct–mid-Mar

Price: adult/child garden only ¥500/300, temple buildings & garden ¥800/600

A major temple of the Rinzai school, Tenryū-ji has one of the most attractive gardens in all of Kyoto, particularly during the spring cherry-blossom and autumn-foliage seasons. The main 14th-century Zen garden, with its backdrop of the Arashiyama mountains, is a good example of shakkei (borrowed scenery). Unfortunately, it's no secret that the garden here is world class, so it pays to visit early in the morning or on a weekday. It was built in 1339 on the old site of Go-Daigo's villa after a priest had a dream of a dragon rising from the nearby river. The dream was seen as a sign that the emperor's spirit was uneasy and so the temple was built as appeasement – hence the name tenryū (heavenly dragon). The present buildings date from 1900. You will find Arashiyama's famous bamboo grove situated just outside the north gate of the temple.

Nanzen-ji

Top choice Buddhist temple in Northern Higashiyama

Details:

86 Fukuchi-chō, Nanzen-ji, Sakyō-ku

http://www.nanzenji.com/

Hours: 8.40am-5pm Mar-Nov, to 4.30pm Dec-Feb

Price: adult/child Nanzen-in ¥300/150, Hōjō garden ¥500/300, San-mon gate ¥500/300, grounds free

This is one of the most rewarding temples in Kyoto, with its expansive grounds and numerous subtemples. At its entrance stands the massive San-mon. Steps lead up to the 2nd story, which has a great view over the city. Beyond the gate is the main hall of the temple, above which you will find the Hōjō, where the Leaping Tiger Garden is a classic Zen garden well worth a look.

Nanzen-ji began as a retirement villa for Emperor Kameyama but was dedicated as a Zen temple on his death in 1291. Civil war in the 15th century destroyed most of the temple; the present buildings date from the 17th century. It operates now as headquarters for the Rinzai school of Zen.

While you're in the Hōjō, you can enjoy a cup of matcha and a sweet while gazing at a small waterfall (¥500; ask at the reception desk of the Hōjō).

Kinkaku-ji

Top choice Buddhist temple in Northwest Kyoto

Details:

1 Kinkakuji-chō, Kita-ku

Hours: 9am-5pm

Price: adult/child ¥400/200

Kyoto's famed 'Golden Pavilion', Kinkaku-ji is one of Japan's best-known sights. The main hall, covered in brilliant gold leaf, shining above its reflecting pond is truly spectacular. Needless to say, due to its beauty, the temple can be packed any day of the year. It's best to go early in the day or just before closing, ideally on a weekday.

The original building was built in 1397 as a retirement villa for shogun Ashikaga Yoshimitsu. His son converted it into a temple. In 1950 a young monk consummated his obsession with the temple by burning it to the ground. The monk's story was fictionalized in Mishima Yukio's The

Golden Pavilion. In 1955 a full reconstruction was completed that followed the original design, but the gold-foil covering was extended to the lower floors.

Shinto Shrines in Kyoto

Fushimi Inari-Taisha

Top choice shinto shrine in Kyoto Station & South Kyoto

Details:

68 Yabunouchi-chō, Fukakusa, Fushimi-ku

Hours: dawn-dusk

With seemingly endless arcades of vermilion torii (shrine gates) spread across a thickly wooded mountain, this vast shrine complex is a world unto its own. It is, quite simply, one of the most impressive and memorable sights in all of Kyoto.

The entire complex, consisting of five shrines, sprawls across the wooded slopes of Inari-san. A pathway wanders 4km up the mountain and is lined with dozens of atmospheric sub-shrines.

Fushimi Inari was dedicated to the gods of rice and sake by the Hata family in the 8th century. As the role of agriculture diminished, deities were enrolled to ensure prosperity in business. Nowadays, the shrine is one of Japan's most popular, and is the head shrine for some 40,000 Inari shrines scattered the length and breadth of the country.

As you explore the shrine, you will come across hundreds of stone foxes. The fox is considered the messenger of Inari, the god of cereals, and the stone foxes, too, are often referred to as Inari. The key often seen in the fox's mouth is for the rice granary. On an incidental note, the Japanese traditionally see the fox as a sacred, somewhat mysterious figure capable of 'possessing' humans – the favored point of entry is under the fingernails.

The walk around the upper precincts of the shrine is a pleasant day hike. It also makes for a very eerie stroll in the late afternoon and early evening, when the various graveyards and miniature shrines along the path take on a mysterious air. It's best to go with a friend at this time.

On 8 April there's a Sangyō-sai festival with offerings and dances to ensure prosperity for national industry. During the first few days in January, thousands of believers visit this shrine as their hatsu-mōde (first shrine visit of the New Year) to pray for good fortune. For info on the shrine's many schedules, see http://inari.jp/en/rite.

Heian-jingū

Shinto Shrine in Northern Higashiyama

Details:

Nishitennō-chō, Okazaki, Sakyō-ku

075-761-0221

Hours: 6am-5pm Nov-Feb, 6am-6pm Mar-Oct, garden 8.30am-4.30pm

Price: garden adult/child ¥600/300

One of Kyoto's more popular sights, this shrine was built in 1895 to commemorate the 1100th anniversary of the founding of the city. The shrine buildings are colorful replicas, reduced to a two-thirds scale, of the Imperial Court Palace of the Heian period (794–1185). About 500m in front of the shrine is a massive steel torii (shrine gate). Although it appears to be entirely separate, this is actually considered the main entrance to the shrine itself.

The vast garden here, behind the shrine, is a fine place for a wander and particularly lovely during the cherry-blossom season. With its large pond, water lilies and Chinese-inspired bridge, the garden is a tribute to the style that was popular in the Heian period. It is well known for its wisteria, irises and beni-shidare-zakura (red weeping cherry blossoms).

One of Kyoto's biggest festivals, the Jidai Matsuri, is held here on 22 October. On 2 and 3 June, Takigi nō is also held here. Takigi nō is a picturesque form of nō (stylized dance-drama performed on a bare stage) staged in the light of blazing fires. Tickets cost ¥3000 if you pay in advance (ask at the Kyoto Tourist Information Center for the location of ticket agencies) or you can pay ¥4000 at the entrance gate.

Kitano Tenman-gū

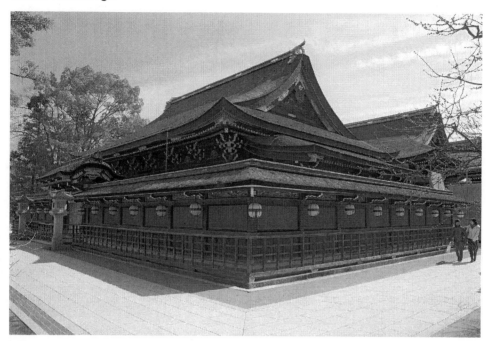

Shinto Shrine in Northwest Kyoto

Details:

Bakuro-chō, Kamigyō-ku

http://www.kitanotenmangu.or.jp/

Hours: 5am-6pm Apr-Sep, 5.30am-5.30pm Oct-Mar

The most atmospheric Shintō shrine in Northwest Kyoto, Kitano Tenman-gū is also the site of Tenjin-San Market, one of Kyoto's most popular flea markets. It's a pleasant spot for a lazy stroll and the shrine buildings themselves are beautiful. The present buildings were built in 1607 by Toyotomi Hideyori; the grounds contain an extensive grove of plum trees, which burst into bloom in early March.

Kitano Tenman-gū was established in 947 to honor Sugawara Michizane (845–903), a noted Heian-era statesman and scholar. It is said that, having been defied by his political adversary Fujiwara Tokihira, Sugawara was exiled to Kyūshū for the rest of his life. Following his death in 903, earthquakes and storms hit Kyoto, and the Imperial Palace was repeatedly struck by lightning. Fearing that Sugawara, reincarnated as Raijin (God of Thunder), had returned from beyond to avenge his rivals, locals erected and dedicated this shrine to him.

Unless you are trying to avoid crowds, the best time to visit is during the Tenjin-san market fair, held on the 25th of each month – December and January are particularly colorful.

Interesting areas in Kyoto

Gion

Top choice area in Southern Higashiyama

Details:

Higashiyama-ku

Gion is the famous entertainment and geisha quarter on the eastern bank of the Kamo-gawa. While Gion's true origins were in teahouses catering to weary visitors to the nearby shrine Yasaka-jinja, by the mid-18th century the area was Kyoto's largest pleasure district. The best way to experience Gion today is with an evening stroll around the atmospheric streets lined with 17th-century traditional restaurants and teahouses lit up with lanterns. Start off on the main street Hanami-kōji, which runs north–south and bisects Shijō-dōri.

At the southern section of Hanami-kōji, many of the restaurants and teahouses are exclusive establishments for geisha entertainment. At the south end you reach Gion Corner and Gion Kōbu Kaburen-jō Theatre (祇園甲部歌舞練場).

If you walk from Shijō-dōri along the northern section of Hanami-kōji and take your third left, you will find yourself on Shimbashi (sometimes called Shirakawa Minami-dōri), which is one of Kyoto's most beautiful streets, especially in the evening and during cherry-blossom season. A bit further north lie Shinmonzen-dōri and Furumonzen-dōri, running east–west. Wander in either direction along these streets, which are packed with old houses, art galleries and shops specializing in antiques – but don't expect flea-market Prices.

Path of Philosophy (Tetsugaku-no-Michi)

Area in Northern Higashiyama

Details:

Sakyō-ku

The Tetsugaku-no-Michi is one of the most pleasant walks in all of Kyoto. Lined with a great variety of flowering plants, bushes and trees, it is a corridor of color throughout most of the year. Follow the traffic-free route along a canal lined with cherry trees that come into spectacular bloom in early April. It only takes 30 minutes to do the walk, which starts at Nyakuōji-bashi, above Eikan-dō, and leads to Ginkaku-ji.

The path takes its name from one of its most famous strollers: 20th-century philosopher Nishida Kitarō, who is said to have meandered lost in thought along the path.

During the day in the cherry-blossom season, you should be prepared for crowds; a night stroll will definitely be quieter.

Ponto-chō

Area in Downtown Kyoto

Details:

Ponto-chō, Nakagyō-ku

There are few streets in Asia that rival this narrow pedestrian-only walkway for atmosphere. Not much to look at by day, the street comes alive at night, with wonderful lanterns, traditional wooden exteriors, and elegant Kyotoites disappearing into the doorways of elite old restaurants and bars.

Ponto-chō is also a great place to spot geiko (geisha) and maiko (apprentice geisha) making their way between appointments, especially on weekend evenings at the Shijō-dōri end of the street. Many of the restaurants and teahouses can be difficult to enter, but several reasonably priced, accessible places can be found. Even if you have no intention of patronizing one of the businesses here, it makes a nice stroll in the evening, perhaps combined with a walk in nearby Gion.

Notable buildings in Kyoto

Kyoto Station

Notable Building in Kyoto Station & South Kyoto

Details:

Karasuma-dōri, Higashishiokōji-chō, Shiokōji-sagaru, Shimogyō-ku

http://www.kyoto-station-building.co.jp/

The Kyoto Station building is a striking steel-and-glass structure – a kind of futuristic cathedral for the transport age – with a tremendous space that arches above you as you enter the main concourse. Be sure to take the escalator from the 7th floor on the east side of the building up to the 11th-floor glass corridor, Skyway (open 10am to 10pm), that runs high above the main concourse of the station, and catch some views from the 15th-floor Sky Garden terrace.

The station building contains several food courts, a foreign currency exchange shop, as well as the JR Isetan Department Store and the Kyoto Tourist Information Center.

Shūgaku-in Rikyū Imperial Villa

Notable Building in Northern Higashiyama

Details:

Shūgaku-in, Yabusoe, Sakyō-ku

075-211-1215

http://www.kunaicho.go.jp/

Hours: tours 9am, 10am, 11am, 1.30pm & 3pm Tue-Sun

One of the highlights of northeast Kyoto, this superb imperial villa was designed as a lavish summer retreat for the imperial family. Its gardens, with their views down over the city, are worth the trouble it takes to visit. The one-hour tours are held in Japanese, with English audio guides free of charge. You must be over 18 years to enter and you will need to bring your passport for ID.

Construction of the villa was begun in the 1650s by Emperor Go-Mizunō, following his abdication. Work was continued by his daughter Akeno-miya after his death in 1680.

The villa grounds are divided into three enormous garden areas on a hillside – lower, middle and upper. Each has superb tea-ceremony houses: the upper, Kami-no-chaya, and lower, Shimo-no-chaya, were completed in 1659, and the middle teahouse, Naka-no-chaya, was completed in 1682. The gardens' reputation rests on their ponds, pathways and impressive use of shakkei (borrowed scenery) in the form of the surrounding hills. The view from Kami-no-chaya is particularly impressive.

You can book tickets in advance at the Imperial Household Agency office or online for morning tours, but for afternoon tours tickets go on sale at the villa from 11am and are available on a first-come, first-served basis until capacity is sold.

Sumiya Pleasure House

Notable Building in Kyoto Station & South Kyoto

Details:

Nishishinyashikiageya-chō 32, Shimogyō-ku

075-351-0024

Hours: 10am-4pm Tue-Sun

Price: adult/child ¥1000/500

Sumiya Pleasure House is the last remaining ageya (pleasure house) in the old Shimabara pleasure quarter. Built in 1641, this stately two-story, 20-room structure allows a rare glimpse into Edo-era nirvana. With its delicate latticework exterior, Sumiya has a huge open kitchen and an extensive series of rooms (including one extravagantly decorated with mother-of-pearl inlay). To visit the 2nd story, you need to join one of the 30-minute tours in Japanese (¥800). Shimabara, a district northwest of Kyoto Station, was Kyoto's original pleasure quarters. At its peak during the Edo period (1603–1868) the area flourished, with more than 20 enormous ageya – magnificent banquet halls where artists, writers and statesmen gathered in a 'floating world' ambience of conversation, art and fornication. Geisha were often sent from their okiya (living quarters) to entertain patrons at these restaurant-cum-brothels. By the start of the Meiji period, however, such activities had drifted north to the Gion district and Shimabara had lost its prominence. There is an English leaflet available and captions throughout.

210

Kyoto State Guest House

Notable Building in Imperial Palace & Around

Details:

Kyoto Gyōen, Kamigyō-ku

http://www8.cao.go.jp/geihinkan/kyoto/kyoto-e.html

Hours: tours at noon Thu-Tue

Price: ¥1500

Built in 2005 to welcome foreign dignitaries, the Kyoto State Guest House is not a must-see sight, unless you have a real interest in architecture. English guided 60-minute tours are a bit painfully slow-moving, taking visitors through room by room of the building, which was designed as a modern interpretation of traditional Japanese architecture. The central garden and koi-filled pond is quite lovely and you do get an insight into the incredible craftsmanship that has gone into every detail.

Tickets can be booked online in advance or you can show up at the west gate In case there are available spots; you need to arrive 30 minutes early for a bag security check.

Landmarks in Kyoto

Tenryū-ji North Gate

Landmark in Arashiyama & Sagano

By exiting Tenryū-ji via this gate and taking a quick left, you'll find yourself almost immediately in the famous Arashiyama Bamboo Grove.

Kyoto City Hall

Landmark in Downtown Kyoto

Details:

cnr Kawaramachi-dōri & Oike-dōri

Built in 1927, this imposing building takes up one block on the corner of Kawaramachi-dōri and Oike-dōri.

Museums in Kyoto

Kyoto Railway Museum

Museum in Kyoto Station & South Kyoto

Details:

Kankiji-chō, Shimogyō-ku

http://www.kyotorailwaymuseum.jp/

Hours: 10am-5.30pm Thu-Tue

Price: adult ¥1200, child ¥200-500, train ride ¥300/100

The Umekoji Steam Locomotive Museum underwent a massive expansion in 2016 to reopen as the Kyoto Railway Museum. This superb museum is spread over three floors showcasing 53 trains, from vintage steam locomotives in the outside Roundhouse Shed to commuter trains and the first shinkansen (bullet train) from 1964. Kids will love the interactive displays and impressive railroad diorama with miniature trains zipping through the intricate landscape. You can also take a 10-minute ride on one of the smoke-spewing choo-choos.

Several of the exhibits have come from Osaka's Modern Transportation Museum, which has now closed. Displays walk visitors through the history of Japanese railway innovation and delve into a new level of detail from railway uniforms and tools to a working level crossing and the inner workings of the ticket machine – buy your ticket, feed it into the machine and watch through the transparent cover! The museum has an open passageway layout so you can peer down on the displays and trains from the upper levels, as well as see city views from the 3rd-floor Skydeck.

Gekkeikan Sake Ōkura Museum

Museum in Kyoto

Details:

247 Minamihama-chō, Fushimi-ku

075-623-2056

http://www.gekkeikan.co.jp/

Hours: 9.30am-4.30pm

Price: adult/child ¥300/100

The largest of Fushimi's sake breweries is Gekkeikan, the world's leading producer of sake. Although most of the sake is now made in a modern facility in Osaka, a limited amount is still handmade in a Meiji-era sakagura (sake brewery) here in Fushimi. The museum is home to a collection of artefacts and memorabilia tracing the 350-year history of Gekkeikan and the sake-brewing process.

There are English captions throughout and your ticket includes a 180ml sake bottle as a gift. If you wish to take a tour of the sake-producing process next door, you need to book in advance for the 15-minute tour in Japanese.

The museum is a 10-minute walk northeast of Chūshojima Station on the Keihan line. It takes about 15 minutes from Sanjo Keihan to Chūshojima Station (¥270). To get to the museum from the station, go right at the north exit, take a right down an unpaved road, a left at the playground, cross the bridge over the canal and follow the road around to the left; the museum is on the left.

Kyoto International Manga Museum

Museum in Downtown Kyoto

Details:

Karasuma-dōri, Oike-agaru, Nakagyō-ku

http://www.kyotomm.jp/

Hours:10am-6pm Thu-Tue

Price: adult/child ¥800/100

Located in an old elementary school building, this museum is the perfect introduction to the art of manga (Japanese comics). It has 300,000 manga in its collection, 50,000 of which are on display in the Wall of Manga exhibit. While most of the manga and displays are in Japanese, the collection of translated works is growing. In addition to the galleries that show both the historical development of manga and original artwork done in manga style, there are beginners' workshops and portrait drawings on weekends.

Visitors with children will appreciate the children's library and the occasional performances of kami-shibai (humorous traditional Japanese sliding-picture shows), not to mention the artificial lawn where the kids can run free. The museum hosts six-month-long special exhibits yearly: check the website for details.

Kyoto Ukiyo-e Museum

Museum in Downtown Kyoto

Details:

2nd fl, Kirihata Bldg, Shijō-dōri, Teramachi Nishiiri, Shimogyō-ku

075-223-3003

http://www.kyoto-ukiyoe-museum.com/

Hours: 10.30am-6.30pm

Price: adult/child ¥600/300

Opened in 2017, this one-room museum displays a selection of ukiyo-e (woodblock prints) by some of Japan's most well-known artists, including Hiroshige Utagawa, Utamaro Kitagawa and Hokusai Katsushika. Ukiyo-e is said to have originated in the 16th century with prints showing the lives of common people in Kyoto, and most of the works shown here are of scenes from Kyoto. The exhibitions change every few months but Japan's most famous ukiyo-e work, Hokusai's The Great Wave off Kanagawa, is permanently on display.

Parks in Kyoto

Arashiyama Bamboo Grove

Top choice park in Arashiyama & Sagano

Details:

Ogurayama, Saga, Ukyō-ku

Hours: dawn-dusk

The thick green bamboo stalks seem to continue endlessly in every direction and there's a strange quality to the light at this famous bamboo grove. It's most atmospheric on the approach to Ōkōchi Sansō villa and you'll be unable to resist trying to take a few photos, but you might be disappointed with the results: photos just can't capture the magic of the place. The grove runs from outside the north gate of Tenryū-ji to just below Ōkōchi Sansō.

Maruyama-kōen

Park in Southern Higashiyama

Details:

Maruyama-chō, Higashiyama-ku

Maruyama-kōen is a favorite of locals and visitors alike. This park is the place to come to escape the bustle of the city center and amble around gardens, ponds, souvenir shops and restaurants. Peaceful paths meander through the trees, and carp glide through the waters of a small pond in the park's center.

For two weeks in early April, when the park's cherry trees come into bloom, the calm atmosphere is shattered by hordes of drunken revelers having hanami (cherry-blossom viewing) parties under the trees. The centerpiece is a massive shidare-zakura cherry tree; this is one of the most beautiful sights in Kyoto, particularly the yozakura (night cherry blossoms) when lit up from below at night. For those who don't mind crowds, this is a good place to observe the

223

Japanese at their most uninhibited. Arrive early and claim a good spot high on the east side of the park, from where you can peer down on the mayhem below.

Kyoto Imperial Palace Park

Park in Imperial Palace & Around

Details:

Kyoto Gyōen, Kamigyō-ku

Hours: dawn-dusk

The Kyoto Imperial Palace (Kyoto Gosho) and Sentō Imperial Palace (Sentō Gosho) are surrounded by the spacious Kyoto Imperial Palace Park, which is planted with a huge variety of flowering trees and open fields. It's perfect for picnics, strolls and just about any sport you can think of. Take some time to visit the pond at the park's southern end, which contains gorgeous carp. The park is most beautiful in the plum- and cherry-blossom seasons (late February and late March, respectively).

The plum arbor is located about midway along the park on the west side. There are several large shidareze-zakura ('weeping' cherry trees) at the north end of the park, making it a great cherry-blossom destination. The park is between Teramachi-dōri and Karasuma-dōri (to the east and west) and Imadegawa-dōri and Marutamachi-dōri (to the north and south).

225

Arashiyama Monkey Park Iwatayama

Park in Arashiyama & Sagano

Details:

8 Genrokuzan-chō, Arashiyama, Ukyō-ku

075-872-0950

http://monkeypark.jp/

Hours: 9am-5pm mid-Mar–Sep, to 4pm Oct–mid-Mar

Price: adult/child ¥550/250

Though it is common to spot wild monkeys in the nearby mountains, here you can encounter them at a close distance and enjoy watching the playful creatures frolic about. It makes for an excellent photo opportunity, not only of the monkeys but also of the panoramic view over Kyoto. Refreshingly, it is the animals who are free to roam while the humans who feed them are caged in a box!

You enter the park near the south side of Tōgetsu-kyō, through the orange torii (shrine gate) of Ichitani-jinja. Buy your tickets from the machine to the left of the shrine at the top of the steps.

Just be warned: it's a steep climb up the hill to get to the monkeys. If it's a hot day, you're going to be drenched by the time you get to the spot where they gather.

Historic buildings in Kyoto

Ōkōchi Sansō

Top choice historic building in Arashiyama & Sagano

Details:

8 Tabuchiyama-chō, Sagaogurayama, Ukyō-ku

Hours: 9am-5pm

Price: adult/child ¥1000/500

This is the lavish estate of Ōkōchi Denjirō, an actor famous for his samurai films. The sprawling gardens may well be the loveliest in all of Kyoto, particularly when you consider the brilliant views eastwards across the city. The house and teahouse are also sublime. Be sure to follow all the trails around the gardens. Hold onto the tea ticket you were given upon entry to claim the matcha (green powdered tea) and sweet that comes with admission.

229

Sentō Imperial Palace

Historic Building in Imperial Palace & Around

Details:

Kyoto Gyōen, Kamigyō-ku

075-211-1215

http://www.kunaicho.go.jp/

Hours: tours 9.30am, 11am, 1.30pm, 2.30pm & 3.30pm Tue-Sun

The Sentō Gosho is the second imperial property located within the Kyoto Imperial Palace Park (the other one is the Imperial Palace itself). The structures are not particularly grand, but the gardens, laid out in 1630 by renowned landscape designer Kobori Enshū, are excellent. Admission is by one-hour tour only (in Japanese; English audio guides are free). You must be over 18 years old and you will need to bring your passport. Your ticket can be printed or shown on a smartphone.

The palace was originally constructed in 1630 during the reign of Emperor Go-Mizunō as a residence for retired emperors. It was repeatedly destroyed by fire and reconstructed; and continued to serve its purpose until a final blaze in 1854, after which it was never rebuilt. Today only two original structures, the Seika-tei and Yūshin-tei teahouses, remain.

You can book tickets in advance at the Imperial Household Agency office or online for morning tours; for afternoon tours tickets go on sale at the palace from 11am and are on a first-come, first-served basis until capacity is sold.

Katsura Rikyū

Historic Building in Arashiyama & Sagano

Details:

Katsura Detached Palace, Katsura Misono, Nishikyō-ku

075-211-1215

http://sankan.kunaicho.go.jp/

Hours: tours 9am, 10am, 11am, 1.30pm, 2.30pm, 3.30pm Tue-Sun

Katsura Rikyū, one of Kyoto's imperial properties, is widely considered to be the pinnacle of Japanese traditional architecture and garden design. Set amid an otherwise drab neighborhood, it is (very literally) an island of incredible beauty. One-hour tours are in Japanese, with English audio guides free of charge. You must be over 18 years and you will need to bring your passport for ID.

The villa was built in 1624 for the emperor's brother, Prince Toshihito. Every conceivable detail of the villa – the teahouses, the large pond with islets and the surrounding garden – has been given meticulous attention.

You can book tickets in advance at the Imperial Household Agency office or online for morning tours but for afternoon tours tickets go on sale at the palace from 11am and are on a first-come, first-served basis until capacity is sold.

It's a 15-minute walk from Katsura Station, on the Hankyū line. A taxi from the station to the villa will cost around ¥600. Alternatively, Kyoto bus 33 stops at Katsura Rikyū-mae stop, which is a five-minute walk from the villa.

Kyoto Imperial Palace

Historic Building in Imperial Palace & Around

Details:

Kyoto Gyōen, Kamigyō-ku

075-211-1215

http://www.kunaicho.go.jp/

Hours: 9am-5pm Apr-Aug, 9am-4.30pm Sep & Mar, 9am-4pm Oct-Feb, last entry 40min before closing, closed Mon

The Kyoto Imperial Palace, known as the Gosho in Japanese, is a walled complex that sits in the middle of the Kyoto Imperial Palace Park. While no longer the official residence of the Japanese emperor, it's still a grand edifice, though it doesn't rate highly in comparison with other attractions in Kyoto. Visitors can wander around the marked route in the grounds where English signs explain the history of the buildings. Entrance is via the main Seishomon Gate where you'll be given a map.

The original imperial palace was built in 794 and was replaced numerous times after destruction by fire. The present building, on a different site and smaller than the original, was constructed in 1855. Enthronement of a new emperor and other state ceremonies are still held here, so at times the palace is closed to the public. Take note: the grounds are covered in gravel stones so wear shoes that are easy to walk in.

Free English guided tours run at 10am and 2pm.

Gardens in Kyoto

Kyoto Botanical Gardens

Gardens in Imperial Palace & Around

Details:

Shimogamohangi-chō, Sakyō-ku

Hours: 9am-5pm, greenhouse 10am-4pm

Price: adult/child gardens ¥200/free, greenhouse ¥200/free

The Kyoto Botanical Gardens occupy 24 hectares and feature over 12,000 plants, flowers and trees. It is pleasant to stroll through the rose, cherry and herb gardens or see the rows of camphor trees and the large tropical greenhouse. This is a good spot for a picnic. It's also the perfect location for a hanami (cherry-blossom viewing) party, and the blossoms here tend to hold on a little longer than those elsewhere in the city.

Shōsei-en

Gardens in Kyoto Station & South Kyoto

Details:

Karasuma-dōri, Shichijō-agaru, Shimogyō-ku

075-371-9210

Hours: 9am-5pm Mar-Oct, to 4pm Nov-Feb

Price: adult/child ¥500/250

About five minutes' walk east of Higashi Hongan-ji, this garden is a peaceful green island in a vast expanse of concrete. While it's not on par with many other gardens in Kyoto, it's worth a visit if you find yourself in need of something to do near Kyoto Station, perhaps paired with a visit to the temple. The lovely grounds, incorporating the Kikoku-tei villa, were completed in 1657.

Murin-an

Gardens in Northern Higashiyama

Details:

Nanzen-ji, Kusakawa-chō, Sakyō-ku

075-771-3909

https://murin-an.jp/en

Hours: 8.30am-6pm

Price: ¥410

Often overlooked by the hordes that descend on the Higashiyama area, this elegant villa was the home of prominent statesman Yamagata Aritomo (1838–1922) and the site of a pivotal 1903 political conference as Japan was heading into the Russo-Japanese War. Built in 1896, the grounds contain well-preserved wooden buildings, including a fine Japanese tearoom. The Western-style annex is characteristic of Meiji-period architecture and the serene garden features small streams that draw water from the Biwa-ko Sosui canal.

For ¥600 you can savor a bowl of frothy matcha (powdered green tea) with a sweet while viewing the shakkei backdrop of the Higashiyama Mountains. It's particularly beautiful in the maple-leaf season of November.

Local flavor on Kyoto's Kiyamachi street

Kiyamachi, Kyoto's biggest nightlife strip, is a one kilometer stretch running parallel to the central Kamo River between two main boulevards, Sanjō and Shijō. On one side of the narrow street, slick-fronted concept restaurants promise cheap drinks and no cover charge. On the other, a shallow, tree-lined canal is laced by arched bridges. It sounds romantic, but the strip is nothing in comparison to Ponto-chō, just one block over.

Ponto-chō is what you want Kyoto nightlife to look like: wooden buildings lit by the soft glow of lanterns and women in kimonos disappearing through low doorways. It can also be exclusive, expensive and intimidating. Many establishments practice ichi gen sen o kotowari, meaning they refuse entry to first time visitors who have not been introduced by a regular customer.

Kiyamachi is the inverse. It is accessible, with big, back-lit signs and touts reassuring that anyone is welcome. But that does not mean that Kiyamachi is completely without local flavor. It is wedged into the cracks, in the alleyways around the noisy cabarets. Tucked away in these authentic haunts is a side of Kyoto that is warm, down-to-earth and stubbornly independent.

Renkon-ya (236 Sanjō-sagaru, Nishi-Kiyamachi; 075-221-1061) has been serving up home-style Kyoto cooking for 60 years. The restaurant's old wooden building dates to the late 19th Century -- one of few such structures in the area. All the produce comes from the local market: the bulbous sora mame (broad beans) grilled in their pods, the tofu lightly battered and fried, the salted, slightly dried karei (flounder). The dishes are prepared in the kitchen behind the counter on a two-burner gas hob by the third-generation proprietor. She shuffles around the bare floor in plastic slippers, greeting customers by name and doing all the cooking and serving herself.

There is more unpretentious food to be found down the street at Takonyūdō (204 Shijō-agaru, Kiyamachi; 075-221-1443). The specialty here is akashiyaki, chunks of octopus enveloped in an egg batter and grilled on a hot plate. Lining the horseshoe shaped counter are bowls of obanzai, a catchall term for quintessentially Kyoto side dishes. Among these are pond snails simmered in soy sauce, fried potato croquettes and beef stewed with devil's root jelly. The mastā and mama-san (the man and the woman, respectively, who run a bar or restaurant) hold court in the central kitchen, dishing up plates along with friendly banter.

For a peek into a more bohemian side of Kyoto, head to Hachimonjiya. Professional photographer Kai Fusayoshi has been running this Kiyamachi bar for 28 years (and has been documenting life in Kyoto for even longer). Piled on the ends of the bar, on tables in the corner and on the floor are mountains of photo books, magazines and exhibition flyers -- the steady accumulation of decades. The bar stools are dangerously unstable and the beer tap rattles violently, but the hard-drinking regulars do not seem to mind -- they are too busy lobbing provocations across the counter. Presiding over all of this is Fusayoshi himself, in jeans and sweatshirt, still boiling water on the stove in a saucepan for every glass of oyuwari (shōchū liquor mixed with hot water), instead of using a kettle.

There is no better place to wind up an evening in Kiyamachi than Eiraku (365 Kamiya-chō, Shijō-agaru; 075-212-2555), otherwise known as the ochazuke bar. Ochazuke is a dish of rice topped with fish, seaweed, pickled plum (or any number of savory toppings), drowned in hot green tea or broth. In Kyoto, the dish is often called bubuzuke, and when a Kyoto native asks if a guest wants to eat bubuzuke, it really means that the person has overstayed and is being politely asked to leave.

For those who would like to finish the night with a belly-warming bowl of ochazuke, Eiraku stays open past dawn. The barman, with shaggy bleached hair and a cotton kimono tied loosely over a t-shirt, believes his bar is the only one of its kind. His endeavor has earned at least one nod of approval from the Ponto-chō version of Kyoto nightlife: a single, signed maiko (apprentice geisha) fan rests on at top shelf -- a sign of patronage.

Kyoto's coffee culture

In a city known for tea and temples, Kyoto is also home to a surprisingly vibrant coffee scene.

Owner-run cafes are flourishing as locals seek peace in a new kind of space, and the best ones build on the city's natural charm, taking into consideration its historic buildings, the quiet side streets and that famous attention to detail that Kyoto artisans have long applied to their work. Hand-painted signs, scalloped awnings and wonderfully restored traditional facades mark the entrances to many of the city's alluring coffee haunts.

The new wave cafe

Daisuke Takayama's Kamogawa Café is one of the many new coffee shops that have swept through Kyoto in the last 10 years, taking both the beverage and the space in which it is consumed very seriously.

The cafe occupies a lofty, second floor space that overlooks a side street near Kyoto's central Kamo River, which runs to the east of the Imperial Palace grounds. The front windows -- checkered panes of coloured and frosted glass -- resemble a Piet Mondrian painting, the floor and tables are made of warm, unstained wood and the menu is hand-drawn.

To really succeed in the Kyoto cafe scene, you need a strong sense of originality," Takayama explained.

But it is the coffee, which Takayama hand roasts daily, that has nudged Kamogawa Café into the upper tier of Kyoto cafes. Left to percolate slowly through a flannel filter, instead of an ordinary paper one, the coffee is thick and strong.

The classic cafe

This particular coffee shop looks like something lifted from the golden age of rail travel between the first and second world wars -- an era of trunks and porters and dressing for the dining car. Long and narrow like a railway carriage, the kissaten has a single counter and richly stained wood paneling.

There is only one man behind the counter, who makes only one cup of coffee at a time. He juggles two fat kettles that take turns boiling on the gas hob. On top of freshly ground, hand-roasted coffee, he adds a little water. He waits; then he adds some more, gently swirling the small glass carafe. Then he waits some more. Before pouring each cup, he gently warms the carafe over an open flame.

A sense of place

New cafes cannot compete with the history of a place like Rokuyōsha, but they can adopt a legacy of a different sort. Take Sarasa Nishijin, housed inside the old Fuji-no-mori Onsen, a former bathhouse from the 1920s.

The coffee shop still looks like an old bathhouse, with wooden latticework and a distinctive, bell-shaped awning. The light-handed renovations kept the original ornate jade and bubble-gum pink tiles intact. A crumbling wall that once separated the men and women's sides of the bath runs down the center of the room, and vintage armchairs are set under the tapered ceiling that rises up to a central chimney.

Another local fixture is the enthusiastically named Café Bibliotic Hello!, installed inside a century-old machiya, a traditional two-story wooden merchant home. The second floor, which would have been the living quarters, is now a loft, and one whole wall is given over to a bookshelf. The first floor, where a shop would had been, retains the exposed wooden beams and showcase windows. But the gloomy atmosphere that young Japanese often attach to old houses has been replaced with a hodgepodge of stylish retro lighting fixtures and convivial chatter.

Not all of Kyoto's popular cafes look to the past for inspiration. Efish, the work of local product designer Shin Nishibori, is entirely in the present. With glass walls that overlook the Kamo River on one side and the Takase canal on the other, it is a prime place to observe the rhythms of the city and its waterways. It is also the kind of place that seamlessly transitions from day to evening, and like many of the city's newer cafes, Efish stays open late, making the most of its riverside location.

The designer's modern, minimal creations furnish the narrow, two-story cafe, and a few of his works are also on sale, including a ceramic coffee roaster shaped like a gourd that works on an ordinary gas range, should you be inspired to brew your own perfect cup.

Sakura season in Kyoto

With Zen gardens, bamboo groves, Buddhist temples and geisha shuffling along cobbled laneways, Kyoto seems to be lifted straight from the scenes of an ancient Japanese woodblock print. And come cherry blossom season -- a national obsession in Japan – the country's cultural heartland is not to be missed. Signaling the arrival of spring, this season sees trees bloom into sakura (cherry blossoms) that line Kyoto's canals, hang low over lakes and transform gardens into blankets of fairy floss.

Cherry blossom philosophy

The cherry blossom is richly symbolic within Japan – it is depicted on the 100-yen coin and was used as a symbol to stoke nationalism during World War II. Many Japanese believe that the blooming of the trees symbolizes the transience of life and is an annual reminder that time is precious. The cherry blossom cycle is seen as a metaphor for life itself – a time to reflect on your achievements and think ahead to your future. Once you have finished philosophizing, indulge in some of Japan's more light-hearted symbolism. Many consumer brands take advantage of this time of year, with many sakura-related products on sale. Try a pastel-pink Sakura Frappuccino at Starbucks or the cherry-flavored white chocolate Sakura Kit Kat.

Hanami

It is unknown exactly when hanami (cherry blossom viewing) first started, but it was mentioned early on, in Shikibu Murasaki's classic Japanese literary work, the Tale of Genji, thought to be written around the 11th or 12th Century. Hanami is an important Japanese custom, when locals break free of their conservative reputation and enjoy a picnic with friends and family under the cherry blossom trees. To partake in a hanami party, grab a bento box and some beer from your nearest combini (convenience store) and head to one of Kyoto's many viewing spots for a Japanese cultural experience of a different kind.

Kyoto's famous cherry blossom spots can get extremely crowded, so make sure you get there early and claim your spot with a picnic rug or tarp. Your reserved piece of plot will be respected, even if you disappear and come back later that day.

Top viewing spots

Kodai-ji is a historic Zen temple located in the scenic Higashiyama area and was one of the first temples to kick off after-dark illuminations (when the gardens are lit by multicolored spotlights), allowing cherry blossom viewing to continue well into the night.

The pedestrian path Tetsugaku-no-Michi, named after 20th-century philosopher Nishida Kataro, stretches for three kilometers alongside a canal in eastern Kyoto and connects Ginkakuji temple to Nanzen-ji temple. This well-known route is lined with cherry trees which are reflected in the still waters, and is an ideal spot to ponder and admire the surrounding natural beauty.

At the base of Kyoto's western mountains, the area of Arashiyama is a main tourist thanks to its swaying bamboo groves and views of stunning foliage. It attracts tourists throughout the year, but really ramps up during cherry blossom season. People crowd the Togetsukyo Bridge (Moon Crossing Bridge) to take in the views, so head away from the main strip to get away from the hordes. At night, the area is lit up for cherry blossom viewing and food stalls are set up with a variety of snacks.

Located in the southern Higashiyama area, Maruyama Koen is usually a good spot to take in some peace and quiet after temple-hopping in Kyoto. However, during cherry blossom season, the park becomes crowded and noisy due to its extremely popular, huge weeping trees.

Best time for viewing

The season -- late March to mid-April -- is relatively short and the blossoming of the trees advances from the south to the north of the country, dubbed the "cherry blossom front". The Japanese Meteorological Agency tracks the progress of the blossoming trees every year and it is reported on the nightly news. Otherwise, the Japan National Tourism Organization also offers forecasts.

Kyoto on a budget

Despite the recent strength of the yen, Kyoto is a bargain compared to cities like London, Paris, New York or Sydney. In fact, for less than you might spend on a good hotel in any of these cities, you can get a comfortable room, eat two good meals, see some incredible sights and have enough left over for a drink in the evening.

Kyoto is packed with reasonably Priced accommodations. For about 8,000 yen you can get a twin room in a mid-range 'business hotel', where rooms are usually small, but spotless and fitted with all the amenities a business traveler would need. Good business hotels in Kyoto include the Toyoko Inn Kyoto Gojo-Karasuma and the Kyoto Palace Side Hotel.

If you do not mind sleeping in a space the size of a roomy telephone booth, then consider one of Kyoto's affordable capsule hotels, which offer sleeping pods just big enough for you and your iPod (bathing facilities are shared and luggage is stored in lockers). You can choose from the ultramodern 9h (Nine Hours) or the wonderfully quirky Capsule Ryokan Kyoto, which offers capsules in the style of a traditional ryokan (Japanese inn). A capsule at these places will set you back between 4,000 and 5,000 yen and Capsule Ryokan Kyoto offers excellent twin rooms from 8,000 yen).

Once you have your accommodation sorted, it is time to explore the city. Kyoto may be Asia's most bicycle-friendly city – it is mostly flat and drivers are relatively sane – so consider renting wheels at a place like Kyoto Cycling Project (from 1,000 yen per day). You will save on bus and subway fares, and be able to move around at will. If you opt for public transport, pick up a one-day bus/subway pass for 1,200 yen.

Surprisingly, some of Kyoto's most impressive attractions are free - such as all four of Kyoto's imperial properties: The Imperial Palace, the Sento Gosho, Shugaku-in Rikyu Detached Palace and Katsura Rikyu Detached Palace. Just bear in mind that you will need to make reservations at the Imperial Household Office, and that people younger than 20 years of age are only allowed into the main property, the Imperial Palace.

If you cannot secure a reservation, there are plenty of other places that are free and can be visited without a booking. One of Kyoto's most beautiful Zen temples, Nanzen-ji, can be toured free of charge (but there is a fee to enter the enclosed rock garden). Likewise, there is no entry fee at Chion-in, which some people call "the Vatican of Pure Land Buddhism". Sitting in the soaring main hall listening to the monks chant is magical. Other free-of-charge temples include Tofuku-ji and Honen-in, an exquisite little temple that many visitors overlook.

After exploring the world of Japanese Buddhism, step back in time and enter the realm of Shinto, Japan's indigenous religion. Almost all Shinto shrines in Kyoto can be visited for free. Fushimi-Inari-Taisha, in the southeast of the city, is one of Japan's most incredible sights, consisting of hypnotic arcades of vermillion torii (Shinto shrine gates) cascading across a green mountainside. You have probably seen pictures – but no camera can capture the atmosphere of this place.

If you fear that eating out in Kyoto will require a second mortgage on your home, you are in for a very pleasant surprise. An excellent sit-down dinner can be had for 1,000 yen per person. And if you want to go cheaper, try a tasty bowl of noodles (ramen, soba or udon) for around 700 yen – try ramen shop Karako in the northern Higashiyama sightseeing district. If you want to experience one of Kyoto's sublime kaiseki (haute-cuisine) restaurants, do like the locals and go at lunch when you can usually get a set meal for around 3,000 yen per person.

At the end of a great day in Kyoto, settle in for a couple glasses of the good stuff (1,200 yen) at a sake bar like Yoramu.

Kōyō: Japan's autumn explosion of color

Literally translated as 'red leaves,' kōyō is to autumn what cherry blossoms are to spring in Japan. Both natural events bring the Japanese out en masse to celebrate the changing seasons, with hanami (cherry blossom viewing) parties in the springtime and momiji-gari (maple leaf viewing) in the fall.

Such festivities are tinged with more fervor in the spring, when the Japan Meteorological Agency tracks predicted blooming dates of cherry blossoms across Japan. Boozy picnics on a mass scale occur in parks boasting cherry blossom trees, as hanami fever grips the land. Because the blooming cycle is so fleeting, this springtime event tends to be more highly anticipated and intensely celebrated. Shops are flooded with cherry blossom merchandise and food, the color pink suddenly popping up in decorative garlands and flower-shaped sweets.

But autumn's kōyō is just as visually stunning and feels less fraught with urgency, as the turning leaves remain on the trees much longer than fluttering cherry blossoms. It also allows more variety in the experience – if you're not particularly fond of picnicking under the trees with ten thousand others (as during cherry blossom season), kōyō affords many opportunities to take in the spectacle by exploring rather than sitting and drinking in a crowded park. Shades of red, vermilion and gold light up forested hillsides, shrine and temple grounds, public gardens and city avenues all over the country.

Though bright-red Japanese maples are most recognizable, many other showy trees burst into color, like the deep golden ginkgo and burnt-orange zelkova trees. Kōyō sets wild hillsides aflame with variegated hues of scarlet while city streets are enlivened by pops of shocking orange. The most popular viewing areas can get crowded with admirers, but it's also possible to take in the color by taking a multi-day trek through the mountains or roaming the paths of an out-of-the-way public garden.

Elevation and temperature dictate the when and where of the brilliant leaves, but the season generally lasts from September to November, beginning in the cooler regions and higher elevations and reaching warmer, more southerly areas last. In fact, autumn is to be one of the best times of the year to visit Japan, as summer's heat and humidity give way to cooler weather.

A few favorite Kōyō spots

The Japan National Tourist Organization highlights viewing spots for the best autumn color according to month, for regions all over Japan – a helpful tool for planning your trip.

Asahidake, Hokkaidō – With a hot spring at the base of this active volcano, Asahidake is part of Daisetsuzan, Hokkaido's largest national park. The leaves here begin turning in September, making the alpine backdrop even more dramatic. It's possible to take one- to two-day treks through the national park, as well as shorter day hikes.

Arashiyama district, Kyoto – Kyoto rolls out the red, leafy carpet during kōyō season, when the city's many temple and shrine grounds look even more elegant. On the outskirts of Kyoto, the Arashiyama district is famous for its autumn color, with mountain views from the Tōgetsukyō bridge and small temples surrounded by colorful trees.

Hakone – A lovely mountain town near Mt Fuji, Hakone is a wonderful destination in its own right. With hot springs, small museums, traditional gardens and a mountain lake, the fall foliage only makes the scenery all the more gorgeous.

Get the latest Japan guide and start planning your picturesque trip

Kaiseki-ryōri: Japanese haute cuisine

Sushi has come a long way from its street-snack origins back in the early 1800s; in 2009, a couple of Tokyo sushi bars each earned three Michelin stars. And while it carries a certain special-occasion cachet internationally, sushi is by no means the Japanese zenith of gastronomy. That honor goes to the cuisine known as kaiseki-ryōri.

With its origins stemming from the delicacies offered to the imperial court, kaiseki-ryōri synthesizes some of the best Japanese values: harmony, balance and an appreciation of the moment. While that might sound pretentiously abstract, a kaiseki meal is truly intended to appeal to all of the senses.

Served in small courses, each dish is prepared with the freshest seasonally-available ingredients, the balance of flavors and textures appreciated not only by the palate, but also visually and experientially. Before allowing that tendril of delicately battered calamari to hit the tongue, a diner should first admire the artistic manner in which the tempura was arranged upon the gold-flecked Japanese paper lining its woven bamboo dish. One should also take in the minimalist beauty of the quiet dining room, and perhaps reflect on the view of the traditional garden outside the sliding screen.

As each course is finished, it is cleared away for presentation of the next, the kaiseki meal a beautiful procession of contrasting tastes and tactile sensations. Lifting the cover of a lacquer bowl might reveal a clear broth with a tiny cube of silken tofu and shreds of chive and citron, followed by a charcoal brazier bearing a small grilled fish, after which an arrangement of candy-coloured dumplings and local wild vegetables might appear on a dish of rustic stoneware. The meal is often finished with a traditional sweet – such as a sticky rice cake in the shape of a purple blossom, with paper-thin slices of pear shaped like leaves.

Kaiseki-ryōri is best exemplified in the restaurants and ryokan (inns) of Kyoto. As the cultural capital of Japan, traditional arts are actively cultivated in the city. Though the formality of the experience can be intimidating to foreigners, enjoying a kaiseki meal in Kyoto is highly accessible and offers a delicious encounter that can't be exported.

If staying in a traditional Kyoto inn, a kaiseki dinner is often included in accommodation rates. In the inn setting, you can consider yourself respectably attired for such a dignified supper if you dress in the cotton kimono provided in your room (bonus: you're dressed in what is essentially a bathrobe and can loosen the sash if you find that the meal was five courses longer than you expected). Alternatively, you could reserve in advance at a highly-regarded establishment like Kikunoi to fully experience the kind of special-occasion atmosphere that befits a first kaiseki-ryōri.

Kyoto's living art of the geisha

Catching a glimpse of a geisha scurrying to an appointment in the narrow streets of Kyoto's Gion entertainment district is a moment of pure magic. With their startling white faces and brilliant kimono, they seem equal parts alien and apparition. If you're like most travelers, you may find it hard to believe your own eyes when you see one of these exquisite beings.

According to most estimates, there are about 1000 geisha in Japan, and many of them live and work in Kyoto, where they are properly known as geiko. Kyoto is also home to tomaiko (apprentice geiko), who are girls between the ages of 16 and 20 who are in the process of completing the four or five years of study it takes to become a fully-fledged geiko. It's easy to tell the difference between the two: Maiko wear elaborate hairpins in their own hair and elaborate kimono, while geiko wear wigs with only the simplest ornamentation (usually just a boxwood comb) and simpler kimono.

A living tradition

The origins of today's geisha (geiko and maiko) can be traced back to the Edo Period (1600–1868), although they became most popular during the Taisho Period (1912–1926). To answer the most common question regarding geisha: they are most definitely not prostitutes. Rather, geisha are highly skilled entertainers, who entertain guests at private parties and dinners. In many ways, geisha are living embodiments of Japanese traditional culture: each one is well versed in traditional dancing, singing, musical instruments and occasionally other arts such as tea ceremony and ikebana (flower arrangement).

An evening of geisha entertainment often begins with an exquisite meal of kaiseki (Japanese haute-cuisine). During the meal, the geisha will chat with guests, pour drinks and light cigarettes. Following dinner, the geisha may dance to music provided by a jikata, who plays the traditional, three-stringed shamisen. Geisha may also engage the guests in a variety of drinking games, at which they excel, almost always resulting in guests getting progressively sozzled.

Geisha events

Considering the cost of a geisha's training and kimono, it's hardly surprising that geisha entertainment is quite expensive: dinner for two guests with one geisha runs about US$700 and parties with a jikata and two or more geisha easily tops US$1000 (making geisha entertainment a better idea for groups of travelers than individuals). These days, some hotels and ryokan in Kyoto offer regular geisha events for guests. If you happen to be in Kyoto in the spring or fall, the geisha dances put on by the city's five geisha districts should be considered must-sees. For those who want to arrange private geisha entertainment, it can be done through private tour companies and high-end ryokan and hotels. Finally, if you spot a woman who looks like a geisha wandering through the tourist districts of Kyoto during the daytime trailed by a photographer, you can be pretty sure she's a tourist who's paid to be made up as a geisha, and not a real maiko or geiko!

Yokohama

Even though it's just a 20-minute train ride south of central Tokyo, Yokohama (横浜) has an appealing flavor and history all its own. Locals are likely to cite the uncrowded, walkable streets or neighborhood atmosphere as the main draw, but for visitors it's the breezy bay front, creative arts scene, multiple microbreweries, jazz clubs and great international dining.

Yokohama is Japan's second largest city, with a soothing bayside location, historic and contemporary architecture, interesting museums, and a booming craft beer industry. It is also home to the art festival Yokohama Triennale, in town again in 2017.

Art and architecture

'Islands, Constellations and Galapagos' is the theme for 2017's Yokohama Triennale. This contemporary art fest runs for three months from 4 August, providing a boost to the city's already vibrant creative scene. Two of the major venues hosting shows during the Triennale are Yokohoma Museum of Art and BankART Studio NYK, both of which are wonderful galleries worth visiting at any time of year.

BankART Studio NYK occupies what was once the warehouse of the NYK shipping line and is typical of the way older pieces of architecture across Yokohama's port area have been adapted for modern use. A short walk away is Minato Mirai 21. With a name meaning 'port future', this area is a bold combination of contemporary and older buildings: the 296m-tall Landmark Tower and the award-winning Ōsanbashi International Passenger Terminal, a graceful promenade designed to reflect the ripples of ocean waves, sit alongside weathered red-brick Akarenga Sōkō (yokohama-akarenga.jp), a series of 19th-century warehouses transformed into a modern shopping mall.

Quirky museums

Minato Mirai 21 is also the location of a couple of fun museums that will particularly appeal if you're travelling with kids or are playful at heart. The Cup Noodles Museum is an imaginatively designed shrine to the inventor of the instant noodle and the Cup Noodle, Momofuku Ando.

The place is popular so arrive early to bag a slot to create a Cup Noodle with your own design of packaging and ingredients.

Another delight is the Hara Model Railway Museum. Displayed here are items from the 6000-piece collection of model trains and railway memorabilia accumulated by Hara Nobutaro, a development engineer, over 80-plus years. The highlight is Ichiban Tetsumo Park, a 30m by 10m diorama that is every kid's dream train set, with over 450m of track and beautifully detailed models. Children can even play at being the chief operator of the trains.

Diverse neighborhoods

There are several other distinct districts to explore around Yokohama.

Yokohama was one of the first ports in Japan to open to international trade (1859), becoming a major gateway for foreign influence. Among the early arrivals were Chinese traders, eventually leading to the establishment of what became Japan's first and largest Chinatown. The area is a 500 sq. meter enclave marked by five brightly decorated 'Pailou' gateways, with red and gold lanterns dangling over narrow lanes lined with over 500 restaurants. A good one to try is Manchinrō Honten, which has been serving up tasty dim sum for over 100 years.

Motomachi-Yamate, meanwhile, offers a chic shopping street overlooked by a wooded bluff where several vintage European-style residences have been preserved. This is where some of the first foreigners took up residence in the city in the late 19th century. Alight at Motomachi-Chūkagai metro station for either Chinatown or Motomachi-Yamate.

Around 2km southwest of Minato Mirai 21, the once red-light district of Koganechō is now populated by young creatives and entrepreneurs who have transformed beneath-the-train-tracks commercial spaces into compact art studios, galleries, shops, cafes and bars. The annual art festival Koganechō Bazaar (koganecho.net) is a free exhibition of street art across the area.

Celebrating craft beer

Raise your glasses for Yokohama's enthusiastic embrace of beer. The city is stacked with microbreweries, such as Bashamichi Taproom and Yokohama Brewery, as well as several other bars, big and small, specializing in quality craft ales from across Japan. Mark your calendars for two annual beer-related events in the city: The Great Japan Beer Festival (beertaster.org) in September, and the Yokohama Oktoberfest held in the Akarenga Sōkō in early October, which features copious quaffing of some 130 different ales.

Make it happen

JR Yokosuka–line trains run to Kamakura from Tokyo (¥920, 56 minutes) via Yokohama (¥340, 27 minutes). Alternatively, the Shōnan Shinjuku line runs from the west side of Tokyo (Shibuya, Shinjuku and Ikebukuro, all ¥920) in about one hour, though some trains require a transfer at Ōfuna, one stop before Kita-Kamakura. For more planning and events information, check out

257

Yokohama Official Visitors' Guide (yokohamajapan.com) and Kamakura City Tourism Association (kamakura-info.jp).

Museums in Yokohama

Cup Noodles Museum

Museum in Yokohama

Details:

2-3-4 Shinkō, Naka-ku

045-345-0918

http://www.cupnoodles-museum.jp/

Hours: 10am-6pm Wed-Mon

Price: adult/child ¥500/free

Dedicated to Momofuku Ando's instant ramen invention, this slickly designed, interactive museum includes a cutesy animated film on the history of the Cup Noodle. The highlight is the chance to design your own Cup Noodle (additional ¥300) by coloring your cup, selecting ingredients and having it air-sealed to take home to enjoy. Even though English signage is sparse, the underlying message of 'Never give up!' and going against the grain is worth the visit, especially for those with kids.

Hara Model Railway Museum

Museum in Yokohama

Details:

2nd fl, Yokohama Mitsui Bldg, 1-1-2 Takashima

Nishi-ku

http://www.hara-mrm.com/english

Hours: 11am-5pm Wed-Mon

Price: adult/child ¥1000/500

The result of Hara Nobutaro's lifelong obsession with trains, this superb collection of model trains and other railway-associated memorabilia is every kid's and train spotter's dream come true. Even if you don't care much for trains, the sheer scale of the collection and beautiful detail of the exhibits is captivating. The highlight is the mammoth gauge-one diorama of moving locomotives where you can act as train driver.

Shin-Yokohama Rāmen Museum

Museum in Yokohama

Details:

2-14-21 Shin-Yokohama

Kohoku-ku

045-471-0503

http://www.raumen.co.jp/ramen

Hours: 11am-10pm Mon-Sat, 10.30am-10pm Sun

Price: adult/child ¥310/100, dishes around ¥900

Nine ramen restaurants from around Japan were hand-picked to sell their wares in this inventive replica of a 1958 shitamachi (downtown district) that's lit to feel like perpetual, festive night-time. It's a short walk from the Shin-Yokohama station – ask for directions at the station's information center. Most of the restaurants offer 'mini' sizes so you can sample a few.

Yokohama Port Museum

Museum in Yokohama

Details:

2-1-1 Minato Mirai

Nishi-ku

045-221-0280

http://www.nippon-maru.or.jp/

Hours: 10am-5pm Tue-Sun

Price: museum & ship adult/child ¥600/300

Explore the docked Nippon Maru, a four-masted barque (built in 1930) that retains many original fittings. As you exit, the comprehensive, and somewhat dry, port museum takes you through the city's port history; kids will love the simulated ship ride.

Galleries in Yokohama

Yokohama Museum of Art

Top choice gallery in Yokohama

Details:

3-4-1 Minato Mirai

Nishi-ku

045-221-0300

http://www.yaf.or.jp/yma

Hours: 10am-6pm, closed Thu

Price: adult/child ¥500/free

The focus of the Yokohama Triennale (2017, 2020), this museum hosts exhibitions that swing between safe-bet shows with European headliners to more daring contemporary Japanese and up-and-coming Southeast Asian artists. There are also permanent works, including by Picasso, Miró and Dalí, in the catalogue.

BankART Studio NYK

Gallery in Yokohama

Details:

3-9 Kaigan-dōri

Naka-ku

045-663-2812

http://www.bankart1929.com/

Hours: cafe 11.30am-5.30pm, gallery hours vary

Price: admission varies

In a former warehouse, this multifloor gallery is a fixture on the local arts scene. It hosts changing exhibitions from local and international artists, and you can sift through flyers for local events over drinks in the 1st-floor cafe before stocking up on art and design books in the excellent attached shop.

Gardens in Yokohama

Sankei-en

Gardens in Yokohama

Details:

58-1 Honmoku-sannotani

Naka-ku

045-621-0634

http://www.sankeien.or.jp/

Hours: 9am-5pm

Price: adult/child ¥500/200

Opened to the public in 1906, this beautifully landscaped garden features walking paths among ponds, 17th-century buildings, several fine tea-ceremony houses and a 500-year-old, three-story pagoda. The inner garden is a fine example of traditional Japanese garden landscaping.

From Yokohama or Sakuragi-chō Station, take bus 8 to Honmoku Sankei-en-mae bus stop (10 minutes).

Parks in Yokohama

Yamashita-kōen

Park in Yokohama

This seaside, landscaped park is perfect for strolling and ship watching. Moored here is the retired luxury 1930 passenger liner Hikawa Maru.

Kamonyama-kōen

Park in Yokohama

Details:

57 Momijigaoka

Hours: 24hr

This small hilltop park is a popular spot for cherry-blossom viewing (hanami) parties in spring.

Zō-no-hana Park

Park in Yokohama

The waterfront Zō-no-hana Park and a series of breezy promenades connect Minato Mirai 21's main attractions.

Notable buildings in Yokohama

Landmark Tower

Notable Building in Yokohama

Details:

2-2-1 Minato Mirai

Nishi-ku

http://www.yokohama-landmark.jp/

Hours: 11am-8pm

Price: adult/child ¥1000/500

Standing an impressive 296m high (70 floors), the Landmark Tower has one of the world's fastest lifts (45km/h). On clear days the 69th-floor Sky Garden observatory affords views to Tokyo and Mt Fuji, and you can get a glimpse into games taking place at Yokohama Stadium.

Ōsanbashi International Passenger Terminal

Notable Building in Yokohama

Details:

1-1-4 Kaigan-dōri

Naka-ku

045-211-2304

https://osanbashi.jp/

Hours: 24hr

Kantei-byō

Temple in Yokohama

Details:

140 Yamashita-chō

Hours: 9am-7pm

Chinatown's heart is this elaborately decorated temple dedicated to Kanwu, the god of business.

Kamakura and Yokohama: two escapes south of Tokyo

Tokyo is dazzling, frenetic and fashionably cool, but there are times when the population crush and non-stop energy turns this urban paradise into a pressure cooker. An easy escape is to head for the seaside in Kamakura and Yokohama, both easy day trips south of Tokyo.

Kamakura

Today known for its relaxed vibe and surf scene, Kamakura once served as Japan's capital (from 1185 to 1333). Venerable Buddhist temples and Shintō shrines nestle amid the verdant hills that surround the town, offering the opportunity for easy hikes followed by foodie shopping and an outdoor hot-spring dip.

Giant Buddha and surfboards

From Kamakura Station, the old-fashioned Enoden line trains rattle three stops past suburban houses to Hase, location of Kamakura's most famous sight: the iconic Daibutsu. This 11.4m bronze statue of Amida Buddha, framed by forested hills and open sky, gazes serenely out to sea from his stone pedestal in the grounds of the 13th-century temple Kōtoku-in.

It's worth lingering in Hase – its quaint streets lined with minka (old wooden houses) are a pleasure to explore. Some of the houses, such as Ichigeya (ichigeya-en.com), have been turned into attractive cafes and gift shops. The hillside terraces and gardens of Hase-dera provide wonderful views of the bay and the surrounding hills. Pad along Yuigahama beach, off which surfers ride the gentle waves, or hop on a board yourself. There are plenty of places to rent equipment, with the folks at the backpackers IZA Kamakura, or the surfer-favorite burger shack Good Mellows, able to clue you into scene.

Hillside hiking

Starting a short distance from the grounds of Kōtoku-in, the Daibutsu Hiking Course is a 3km trail that leads up into the hills to connect with Kita-Kamakura. It's an easy and shaded route and along the way you can pause at the lovely Itsuki Garden (itsuki-garden.com), a cafe with multiple brick terraces swathed in forest greenery. Near the Kamakura end of the trail, follow the signs to Zeniarai-benten, a cave shrine dedicated to Benten, the goddess of good fortune. Join locals here in the ritual of placing your money into a bamboo basket and giving it a wash in the spring water (zeniarai translates as 'coin washing'), said to bring on financial success.

Shopping and local eats

Flush with the thought of extra cash, indulge in some retail therapy along the lively shopping street Komachi-dōri, which runs from Kamakura Station towards the historic shrine Tsurugaoka Hachiman-gū. Among the souvenirs to look out for are Hato Sable, dove-shaped butter cookies sold by Toshimaya; and freshly made sembei (rice crackers) at Kamakura Ichibanya. For tasty breads and baked goods, search out hippy-trippy Paradise Alley Bread & Co (cafecactus5139.com/paradisealley) in the daily Kamakura Farmers Market, a 10-minute walk south of the station towards the beach. Continue in this direction and then north to locate the rustic restaurant Bonzō. Such is the quality of its handmade soba (buckwheat noodles), the restaurant has been awarded a Michelin star.

Soak under the stars

Having hiked and eaten your way around Kamakura, hop back on the Enoden line to Inamuragasaki. A three-minute walk from the station, facing the beach, is Inamuragasaki Onsen (inamuragasaki-onsen.com), where the soothing spa waters are coloured black with minerals. For ¥1400 you can blissfully relax in a giant rotemburo (open-air bath) while gazing up at the starry skies.

Osaka

If Kyoto was the city of the courtly nobility and Tokyo the city of the samurai, then Osaka (大阪) was the city of the merchant class. Japan's third-largest city is a place where things have always moved a bit faster, where people are a bit brasher and interactions are peppered with playful jabs – and locals take pride in this.

Osaka is not a pretty city in the conventional sense – though it does have a lovely river cutting through the center – but it packs more color than most. The acres of concrete are cloaked in dazzling neon; shopfronts are vivid, unabashed cries for attention. This is not a city that prefers to dress all in black.

Above all, Osaka is a city that loves to eat: it's unofficial slogan is kuidaore ('eat until you drop'). It really shines in the evening, when it seems that everyone is out for a good meal – and a good time.

Every trip does not have to be about ticking off a sightseeing list. Some of the best destinations are seen by getting under its skin to experience it like a local -- and a visit to Osaka, Japan's third largest city after Tokyo and Yokohama, is a prime example. While it does have a national art museum, a castle and an aquarium, really discovering this city is a lesson in experiential travel. Chowing down on local dishes and enjoying a beer with boisterous, good-humored Osakans at the baseball will teach you more about Japanese culture than any museum or temple.

The locals

People who live in Osaka tend to shed the conservatism that is found elsewhere in Japan -- perhaps owing to its prosperity as an arts, theatre and cultural hub at one time -- and the first place you will notice this is on the subway. Elderly ladies laugh together sweetly, teenagers stand in groups and poke fun at each other while businessman bark angrily on cell phones in animated discussion. Bucking the Japanese train etiquette seen elsewhere in the country, passengers do not speak in hushed tones while staring at the ground and the no-cell phone sign is rarely adhered to. Osakans are full of life and down-to-earth, so whether you are dining out, grabbing a beer or just asking for directions, you will find that it is easy to strike up a conversation with the city's friendly and forward locals.

Eat and be merry

Osaka is known as the food capital of Japan with fresh seafood from Osaka Bay and produce from the surrounding mountains, and was referred to as 'Japan's kitchen' during the Edo Period (1601-1867) as essential goods were sent here from all over the country to be shipped worldwide from its busy port.

Osakans are passionate about feasting and even have their own expression to describe it, kuidaore: 'to eat oneself bankrupt'. There are plenty of places to gorge yourself in the city, and while Osaka does have an abundance of high-end international and Japanese dining options, most will not have you filing for bankruptcy just yet. The city is known for its traditional cheap eats and any trip to Osaka would not be complete without sampling what's on offer.

Takoyaki (dumplings filled with octopus) is a delicacy that originated in Osaka, and you will find little takeaway shopfronts throughout the city, with the best in the Dotombori district in minami (the south of the city). Order yourself half-a-dozen takoyaki topped with mayonnaise and a thick sauce similar to Worcestershire, stab one with your toothpick and shovel it into your mouth. Chomping into one of these piping hot dumplings will inevitably have you scalding the roof of your mouth, but it is all part of the experience.

Okonomiyaki, a savory-style pancake that translates roughly to 'as you like it', is another Osakan favorite. It can be made with a variety of ingredients which, when done Osaka-style, are all scrambled together with batter and cabbage before hitting the grill. Choose your own ingredients from tender squid, plump prawns or juicy pork, topped off with bonito (fish) flakes, a thick brown okonomiyaki sauce and mayonnaise. The best spots to try okonomiyaki are the tiny 'mom and pop' operations that are full of history and authentic atmosphere, where you will feel as though you are dining in someone's home. Try popular Tengu (Toyosaki 3-15-19; 06-6372-7676) near Nakatsu station. Or jump off at Dobutsuen Mae station on the Midosuji and Sakaisuji lines, head into the covered arcade and ask around for one of the best okonomiyaki spots in the city -- Chitose (06-6631-6002).

Dotombori

Tokyo may be known for its neon and nightlife, but Osaka has its own slice of madness -- and it is called Dotombori. All the action in this southern district concentrates around the Dotombori canal, Dotombori street and on the Ebisubashi bridge. It is best explored on a weekend once the sun goes down, when it takes on a B-grade horror movie atmosphere with giant mechanical moving crabs, oversized hot dogs, puffer fish and cows hanging overhead from buildings among flashing neon and coloured billboards. On ground level, crowds wander the strip taking snaps of convincing plastic food models in front of restaurants, hawkers squeal about meal deals and spiky bleached-blonde Japanese men in suits attempt to woo young women to the 'host' bars nearby (male versions of the hostess bar). Come here to take it all in, grab a cheap ramen (noodle dish in broth) from the open-air 24-hour Kinryu Ramen street stall (Dotombori 1-7-26; 06-6211-3999; you can't miss the giant dragons on the roof) and people-watch for hours.

Beer and baseball

Two things close to many Osakans' hearts, and essential pursuits for any stopover in this town, are beer and baseball. The summer season from June to September sees beer gardens popping up all over the city, typically located on rooftops of hotel buildings like the Ramada and department stores like Hanshin. Usually the offer is all you can drink (nomihodai) (beer and spirits, but most opt for large frothy lagers) and eat (tabehodai) for about 3,500 yen – guaranteeing a rowdy night out.

Another good spot for experiencing the city's spirit is at a baseball game during the March to October season where locals are at the height of their boisterousness. The majority of Osakans are Hanshin Tiger fans and are known as the country's most dedicated and fanatical fans. Catch baseball fever at a game at Koshien stadium, a 20-minute train ride from Osaka on the Kobe line, and hang out with fans amid of barrage of chants, trumpets, Tigers flags waving in the air and thousands of balloons being released at the seventh inning.

Museums in Osaka

National Museum of Ethnology

Top choice museum in Osaka

Details:

10-1 Senri Expo Park

Suita

06-6876-2151

http://www.minpaku.ac.jp/

Hours: 10am-5pm, closed Wed

Price: adult/child ¥420/110

This ambitious museum showcases the world's cultures, showing them to be the continuous (and tangled) strings that they are. There are plenty of traditional masks, textiles and pottery but also Ghanaian barbershop signboards, Bollywood movie posters and even a Filipino jeepney. Don't miss the music room, where you can summon street performances from around the globe via a touch panel. There are also exhibits on Okinawan history and Japan's indigenous Ainu culture. There's English signage but the audio guide gives more detail.

The museum is in Senri Expo Park (Banpaku-kinen-koen), a 10-minute walk from the monorail station (cross the bridge). The Midō-suji and Tanimachi subway lines intersect with the Osaka Monorail; so does the Hankyū Kyoto line.

Momofuku Andō Instant Ramen Museum

Museum in Osaka

Details:

8-25 Masumi-cho

Ikeda

072-752-3484

http://www.instantramen-museum.jp/

Hours: 9.30am-4pm, closed Tue

From its humble invention in 1958 by Andō Momofuku, (1910–2007; later chair of Nissin Foods), instant rāmen has become a global business and one of Japan's most famous exports. Exhibits here illustrate the origin of Cup Noodles and how they're made; there's also a 'tunnel' of Nissin products that showcases a half-century of package design. The highlight, however, is getting to create your own custom blend Cup Noodles to take away (¥300), including decorating the cup.

Get the free English-language audio guide (¥2000-yen deposit). Expect long queues at weekends. It's about a 10-minute walk from the station. Take the east exit and head down the stairs; go left and then right at the small tourist information center, and the museum will be on your right shortly.

Osaka Museum of History

Museum in Osaka

Details:

4-1-32 Ōte-mae

Chūō-ku

http://www.mus-his.city.osaka.jp/

Hours: 9.30am-5pm, to 8pm Fri, closed Tue

Price: adult/child ¥600/400, combined with Osaka Castle ¥900

Built above the ruins of Naniwa Palace (c 650), visible through the ground floor, this museum tells Osaka's story from the era of this early palace to the early 20th century. English explanations are pretty sparse, though much of the displays are highly visible, including a walk-through recreation of old city life. You can also rent an English-language audio guide (¥200). There are great views of Osaka-jō from the 10th floor.

The museum is just southwest of the castle park, in a sail-shaped building adjoining the NHK Broadcast Center.

Notable buildings in Osaka

Osaka-jō

Top choice castle in Osaka

Details:

1-1 Osaka-jō

Chūō-ku

http://www.osakacastle.net/

Hours: 9am-5pm, to 7pm Aug

Price: grounds/castle keep free/¥600, combined with Osaka Museum of History ¥900

After unifying Japan in the late 16th century, General Toyotomi Hideyoshi built this castle (1583) as a display of power, using, it's said, the labor of 100,000 workers. Although the present structure is a 1931 concrete reconstruction (refurbished in 1997), it's nonetheless quite a sight, looming dramatically over the surrounding park and moat. Inside is an excellent collection of art, armor, and day-to-day implements related to the castle, Hideyoshi and Osaka. An 8th-floor observation deck has 360-degree views.

Hideyoshi's original granite structure was said to be impregnable, yet it was destroyed in 1614 by the armies of Tokugawa Ieyasu (the founder of the Tokugawa shogunate). Ieyasu had the castle rebuilt – using the latest advancements to create terrifically imposing walls of enormous stones. The largest stones are estimated to weigh over a 100 tons; some are engraved with the crests of feudal lords.

There are 13 structures, including several turrets, that remain from this 17th-century reconstruction. Osaka citizens raised money themselves to rebuild the main keep; in 1931 the new tower was revealed, with glittering gold-leaf tigers stalking the eaves.

At night the castle is lit with floodlights (and looks like a ghostly structure hovering above ground). Visit the lawns on a warm weekend and you might catch local musicians staging casual shows. The castle and park are at their colorful best (and most crowded) in the cherry-blossom and autumn-foliage seasons.

Abeno Harukas

Notable Building in Osaka

Details:

1-1-43 Abeno-suji

Abeno-ku

http://www.abenoharukas-300.jp/

Hours: observation deck 9am-10pm

Price: observation deck ¥1500

This Cesar Pelli–designed tower, which opened in March 2014, is Japan's tallest building (300m, 60 storeys). It houses Japan's largest department store (Kintetsu, floors B2–14), the Abeno Harukas Art Museum, a hotel, offices and restaurants. The observatory on the 16th floor is free, but admission is required for the top-level Harukas 300 observation deck, which has 360-degree views of the whole Kansai region through windows that run several storeys high. There's also an open-top atrium up here.

Although Abeno Harukas is Japan's tallest building, the tallest structure is Tokyo Sky Tree, at 634m.

Umeda Sky Building

Notable Building in Osaka

Details:

1-1-88 Ōyodonaka, Kita-ku

Hours: observation decks 10am-10.30pm, last entry 10pm

Price: ¥1000

Osaka's landmark Sky Building (1993) resembles a 40-storey, space-age Arc de Triomphe. Twin towers are connected at the top by a 'floating garden' (really a garden-free observation deck), which was constructed on the ground and then hoisted up. The 360-degree city views from here are breathtaking day or night. Getting there is half the fun – an escalator in a see-through tube takes you up the last five storeys (not for vertigo sufferers). The architect, Hara Hiroshi, also designed Kyoto Station.

The building is reached via an underground passage, a short walk north of Osaka and Umeda stations.

Kani Dōraku Honten

Notable Building in Osaka

Details:

1-6-18 Dōtombori

Chūō-ku

You can't miss the giant animated crab that marks the entrance to Kani Dōraku Honten, which is, of course, a crab restaurant. The shop sells tasty crab sushi rolls (from ¥1200) to go out front.

Parks in Osaka

Triangle Park

Park in Osaka

Details:

Nishi-Shinsaibashi

Chūō-ku

In the middle of Ame-Mura is Triangle Park, an all-concrete 'park' with benches for sitting and watching the fashion parade. Come night, it's a popular gathering spot.

Naka-no-shima-kōen

Park in Osaka

Details:

Naka-no-shima

Kita-ku

Osaka's first public park, created in 1891 at the eastern end of Naka-no-shima, is a good place for an afternoon stroll or picnic lunch.

Notable areas in Osaka

Amerika-Mura

Top choice area in Osaka

Details:

Nishi-Shinsaibashi

Chūō-ku

http://americamura.jp/

West of Midō-suji, Amerika-Mura is a compact enclave of hip, youth-focused and offbeat shops, plus cafes, bars, tattoo and piercing parlors, nightclubs, hair salons and a few discreet love hotels. In the middle is Triangle Park, an all-concrete 'park' with benches for sitting and watching the fashion parade. Come night, it's a popular gathering spot.

Around the neighborhood, look for street lamps like stick-figure people, some painted by artists; the Peace on Earth mural (1983), painted by Osaka artist Seitaro Kuroda, and, of course, a mini Statue of Liberty.

Ame-Mura owes its name to shops that sprang up after WWII, selling American goods such as Zippo lighters and T-shirts.

Dōtonbori

Top choice area in Osaka

Details:

www.dotonbori.or.jp

Highly photogenic Dōtombori is the city's liveliest night spot and center of the Minami (south) part of town. Its name comes from the 400-year-old canal, Dōtombori-gawa, now lined with pedestrian walkways and a riot of illuminated billboards glittering off its waters. Don't miss the famous Glico running man sign. South of the canal is a pedestrianized street that has dozens of restaurants vying for attention with the flashiest of signage.

For the best views, head to Ebisu-bashi, the bridge at the western end of the strip.

Shin-Sekai

Area in Osaka

Details:

Naniwa-ku

A century ago, Shin-Sekai ('new world') was home to an amusement park that defined cutting edge. Now this entertainment district mixes down-on-its-heels with retro cool. It's centered around the crusty, trusty, 103m-high steel-frame tower Tsūten-kaku – built 1912, rebuilt 1956 – and surrounded by ancient pachinko and mahjong parlors that draw some truly down-and-out characters. At the same time, Shin-Sekai draws plenty of visitors for nostalgia and cheap eateries behind over-the-top signage, especially for kushikatsu (deep-fried meat and vegetables on skewers).

Shinto shrines in Osaka

O-hatsu Ten-jin

Shinto Shrine in Osaka

Details:

2-5-4 Sonezaki

Kita-ku

06-6311-0895

http://www.tuyutenjin.com/

Hours: 6am-midnight

Hiding in plain sight amid the skyscrapers of Umeda, this 1300-year-old shrine owes its fame to one of Japan's best-known tragic plays (based on true events). Star-crossed lovers O-hatsu, a prostitute, and Tokubei, a merchant's apprentice, committed double suicide here in 1703, to remain together forever in the afterlife rather than live apart. The current shrine was constructed in 1957 (after WWII destroyed the previous one); it's popular with couples, who come to pray for strength in love – and happier endings.

The shrine is just southeast of Ohatsutenjin-dōri arcade. There's a flea market here the first Friday of each month.

Sumiyoshi Taisha

Shinto Shrine in Osaka

Details:

2-9-89 Sumiyoshi

Sumiyoshi-ku

http://www.sumiyoshitaisha.net/

Hours: dawn-dusk

Dedicated to Shintō deities of the sea and sea travel, this graceful shrine was founded in the early 3rd century and is considered the headquarters for all Sumiyoshi shrines in Japan. The buildings are faithful replicas of the ancient originals, with a couple that date back to 1810, and the grounds are crisscrossed by a tree- and lantern-lined waterway spanned by a bright orange drum bridge. It's a rare Shintō shrine that predates the influence of Chinese Buddhist architectural styles.

The Hankai line tram from Tennōji stops right in front of the torii (Shintō shrine gate).

Imamiya Ebisu-jinja

Shinto Shrine in Osaka

Details:

1-6-10 Ebisu-nishi

Naniwa-ku

06-6643-0150

http://www.imamiya-ebisu.jp/

Hours: 9am-5pm

Nicknamed 'Ebessan', this famous shrine is said to have been founded by Japan's most revered historical figure, the priest-prince Shotoku-taishi, c AD 600. Though many deities have been worshiped here over the centuries, it is now considered the home of the Shintō god of commerce (making the shrine popular with business owners). It hosts the Tōka Ebisu festival each January.

Buddhist temples in Osaka

Hōzen-ji

Buddhist Temple in Osaka

Details:

1-2-16 Namba

Chūō-ku

http://houzenji.jp/

This tiny temple hidden down a narrow alley houses a statue of Fudō Myō-ō (a deity of esoteric Buddhism), covered in thick moss. It's a favorite of people employed in mizu shōbai ('water trade' – a euphemism for the sexually charged night world), who pause before work to throw some water on the statue.

Hōzen-ji Yokochō, the alley filled with traditional restaurants and bars, runs between the temple and the Sennichi-mae shopping arcade.

Shitennō-ji

Buddhist Temple in Osaka

Details:

1-11-18 Shitennō-ji

Tennōji-ku

http://www.shitennoji.or.jp/

Hours: 8.30am-4.30pm Apr-Sep, to 4pm Oct-Mar

Price: adult/student/child ¥300/200/free

Shitennō-ji is one of the oldest Buddhist temples in Japan, said to be founded (in 593) by priest-prince Shotoku-taishi (who first spread Buddhism in Japan). Only the big stone torii (Shintō shrine gate) is original, the oldest of its kind in the country (1294). It's free to see the gate and to wander most of the expansive (though not terribly interesting) grounds. Admission is required to visit the main hall and the five-story pagoda, which (unusually) you can climb up.

Worth a visit is the Honbō-teien strolling garden here (admission extra).

On the 21st and 22nd of each month is a very good flea market outside the temple, with antiques and secondhand goods, including old kimono.

Nagoya

Home-proud Nagoya (名古屋), birthplace of Toyota and pachinko (a pinball-style game), is a manufacturing powerhouse. Although Nagoya's GDP tops that of many small countries, this middle child has grown accustomed to life in the shadow of its bigger brothers, Tokyo and Kansai.

In contrast to its industrial core, well-maintained parks and green spaces prevail in the inner wards. Nagoya has cosmopolitan aspects including some fantastic museums, significant temples and excellent shopping, and Nagoyans take pride in the unpretentious nature of their friendly, accessible city.

In spite of all this, the city still struggles to shake its reputation among Japanese (many who've never visited) as the nation's most boring metropolis. I 're here to disagree.

In a prime spot between Tokyo and Kyoto/Osaka on the Tōkaidō shinkansen line, Nagoya is the gateway to Chūbu's big mountain heart and a great base for day trips.

Museums in Nagoya

JR SCMAGLEV & Railway Park

Top choice museum in Nagoya

Details:

Kinjofuto 3-2-2

050-3772-3910

http://museum.jr-central.co.jp/

Hours: 10am-5.30pm Wed-Mon

Price: adult/child ¥1000/500, shinkansen simulator ¥500

Trainspotters will be in heaven at this fantastic hands-on museum. Featuring actual maglev (the world's fastest train – 581km/h), shinkansen, historical rolling stock and rail simulators, the massive museum offers a fascinating insight into Japanese postwar history through the development of a railroad like no other. The 'hangar' is 20 minutes from Nagoya on the Aonami line, found on the Taiko-dōri side of JR Nagoya Station.

Toyota Exhibition Hall

Museum in Nagoya

Details:

1 Toyota-chō

0565-29-3345

http://www.toyota.co.jp/en/about_toyota/facility/toyota_kaikan

Hours: 9.30am-5pm Mon-Sat, tours 11am

See up to 20 shiny examples of the latest automotive technology hot off the production line and witness first-hand how they're made here at Toyota's global HQ. Fascinating two-hour tours of Toyota Motor Corporation's main factory begin at the Exhibition Hall, with many exhibits fully revamped recently. Visit the museum any time it's open but daily tours must be pre-booked from two weeks to three months in advance. Check the website for full Details:.

Allow two hours to get to Toyota city from central Nagoya; refer to the website for directions and reservations.

Nagoya City Science Museum

Museum in Nagoya

Details:

2-17-1 Sakae

052-201-4486

http://www.ncsm.city.nagoya.jp/

Hours: 9.30am-5pm Tue-Sun

Price: adult/child ¥800/500

This hands-on museum claims the world's largest dome-screen planetarium with some seriously out-of-this-world projection technology. There's also a tornado lab and a deep-freeze lab complete with indoor aurora. Despite scheduled shows being kid-centric and in Japanese, the cutting-edge technology of this impressive, centrally located facility is worth experiencing.

Gardens in Nagoya

Noritake Garden

Gardens in Nagoya

Details:

3-1-36 Noritake-shinmachi

052-561-7290

http://www.noritake.co.jp/

Hours: 10am-6pm Tue-Sun

Pottery fans will enjoy a stroll around Noritake Garden, the 1904 factory grounds of one of Japan's best-known porcelain makers, featuring remnants of early kilns and the pleasant Noritake Gallery. You can also glaze your own dish in the Craft Centre & Museum, which demonstrates the production process. The 'Box Outlet Shop' has ironically unboxed wares at discounted Prices. English signs throughout.

Tokugawa-en

Gardens in Nagoya

Details:

1001 Tokugawa-chō

052-935-8988

http://www.tokugawaen.city.nagoya.jp/

Hours: 9.30am-5.30pm Tue-Sun

Price: adult/senior ¥300/100

This delightful Japanese garden adjacent to the Tokugawa Art Museum was donated by the Tokugawa family to Nagoya city in 1931, but destroyed by bombing in 1945. From that time until a three-year restoration project was completed in 2004, the site was used as a park. Water is its key element – there's a lake, river, bridges and waterfall. Each spring 2000 peonies and irises burst into bloom, and maples ignite in the autumn.

Galleries in Nagoya

Tokugawa Art Museum

Top choice gallery in Nagoya

Details:

1017 Tokugawa-chō

052-935-6262

http://www.tokugawa-art-museum.jp/english

Hours: 10am-5pm Tue-Sun

Price: adult/child ¥1200/500

A must for anyone interested in Japanese culture and history, this museum has a collection of over 10,000 pieces that includes National Treasures and Important Cultural Properties once belonging to the shogun family. A Priceless 12th-century scroll depicting The Tale of Genji is usually locked away, except during a short stint in late November; the rest of the year, visitors must remain content with a video.

Treasure Hall

Gallery in Nagoya

Atsuta-jingū's Treasure Hall displays a changing collection of over 4000 Tokugawa-era swords, masks and paintings.

Notable buildings, shrines and temples in Nagoya

Ōsu Kannon

Buddhist Temple in Nagoya

Details:

2-21-47 Osu

Naka-ku

052-231-6525

http://www.osu-kannon.jp/

Hours: 24hr

The much-visited Ōsu Kannon temple traces its roots back to 1333. The temple, devoted to the Buddha of Compassion, was moved to its present location by Tokugawa Ieyasu in 1610, although the current buildings date from 1970. The library inside holds the oldest known handwritten copy of the kojiki – the ancient mythological history of Japan.

Nagoya City Archives

Historic Building in Nagoya

Details:

1-3 Shirakabe

Higashi-ku

052-953-0051

Hours: 9am-5pm Tue-Sun

Built in 1922 this grand Taisho-era Court of Appeal now houses the city archives. While the archives themselves are difficult to navigate for non-Japanese speakers, the attractive neo-baroque building, with its fine stained-glass ornamentation, is worth a look.

Oasis 21

Landmark in Nagoya

Details:

1-11-1 Higashi-sakura

Higashi-ku

052-962-1011

http://www.sakaepark.co.jp/

Oasis 21 is a bus terminal and transit hub with a difference. Its iconic 'galaxy platform' – an elliptical glass-and-steel structure filled with water for visual effect and cooling purposes – caused quite a stir when it was first built. Feel free to climb the stairs and walk around it while you're waiting for your next ride; it's most fun at night when it's adventurously lit.

Midland Square

Landmark in Nagoya

Details:

4-7-1 Meieki

052-527-8877

http://www.midland-square.com/english

Hours: shops 11am-8pm, restaurants 11am-11pm

Nagoya's tallest building (247m) houses Toyota's corporate HQ and showroom, boutique shopping on the lower floors and a beehive of offices in the middle. On levels 44 to 46 is Sky Promenade, Japan's tallest open-air observation deck.

Nagoya-jō

Castle in Nagoya

Details:

1-1 Honmaru

052-231-1700

http://www.nagoyajo.city.nagoya.jp/

Hours: 9am-4.30pm

Price: adult/child ¥500/free

The original structure, built between 1610 and 1614 by Tokugawa Ieyasu for his ninth son, was levelled in WWII. Today's castle is a concrete replica (with elevator) completed in 1959. Renovations are ongoing. On the roof, look for the 3m-long gilded shachi-hoko – legendary creatures possessing a tiger's head and carp's body. Inside, find treasures, an armor collection and the histories of the Oda, Toyotomi and Tokugawa families. The beautiful year-round garden, Ninomaru-en (二の丸園) has a number of pretty teahouses.

Painstaking reconstruction of the Honmaru Palace (1624–44) using traditional materials and methods commenced in 2009. The project is scheduled for completion in 2018.

Sky Promenade

Viewpoint in Nagoya

Details:

4-7-1 Meieki

052-527-8877

http://www.midland-square.com/

Hours: 11am-9.30pm

Price: adult/child ¥750/500

On levels 44 to 46 of Midland Square, Sky Promenade features Japan's tallest open-air observation deck and a handful of high-altitude, high-Priced eats. Reach them via adventurously lit passageways.

Atsuta-jingū

Shinto Shrine in Nagoya

Details:

1-1-1 Jingū

052-671-4151

http://www.atsutajingu.or.jp/

Although the current buildings were completed in 1966, Atsuta-jingū has been a shrine for over 1900 years and is one of the most sacred Shintō shrines in Japan. Nestled among ancient cypress, it houses the sacred kusanagi-no-tsurugi (grass-cutting sword), one of the three regalia that, according to legend, were presented to the Imperial Family by the sun goddess Amaterasu-Ōmikami. There's a changing collection of over 4000 Tokugawa-era swords, masks and paintings on display in the Treasure Hall.

Sapporo

Japan's fifth-largest city, and the prefectural capital of Hokkaidō, Sapporo (札幌) is a dynamic urban center that offers everything you'd want from a Japanese city: a thriving food scene, stylish cafes, neon-lit nightlife, shopping galore – and then some. While many travelers see the city as a transit hub from which to access Hokkaidō's mountains and hot springs, there are enough worthwhile attractions to keep you here for days. Summer is the season for beer and food festivals. In February, despite the bitter cold, Sapporo's population literally doubles during the famous Snow Festival.

Museums in Sapporo

Ōkura-yama Ski Jump Stadium

Museum in Sapporo

Details:

1274 Miyano-mori, Chūō-ku

011-641-8585

http://www.sapporowintersportsmuseum.com/

Hours: 8.30am-6pm May-Oct, 9am-5pm Nov-Apr

Price: combined lift & museum ticket ¥1000

This ski-jump slope was built on the side of Ōkura-yama for the 1972 Sapporo Winter Games. At 133.6m it's just slightly shorter than Sapporo TV Tower, with a 33-degree incline. What would it feel like to whiz down that? You can hazard a guess after taking the rickety old lift up to the top and staring down the slope. Keep that image in mind when you try the highly amusing computerized simulator in the museum below.

There are a few other simulators in the museum, as well as photos and equipment from the 1972 Games – which show just how far winter sports technology (and fashion!) has come in the last 45 years.

The stadium is actually still in use and if you're lucky, you might catch a practice session.

To reach Ōkura-yama, take the Tōzai subway line to Maruyama Kōen (円山公園), and then take exit 2 for the Maruyama bus terminal. Next, take bus 14 to Ōkurayama-kyōgijō-iriguchi (大倉山競技場入り口; ¥210, 15 minutes); from here, it's a 10-minute walk uphill to the stadium.

Sapporo Beer Museum

Museum in Sapporo

Details:

N7E9 Higashi-ku

011-748-1876

http://www.sapporoholdings.jp/english/guide/sapporo/

Hours: 11.30am-8pm

This legendary Sapporo attraction is in the original Sapporo Beer brewery, a pretty, ivy-covered brick building. There's no need to sign up for the tour; there are plenty of English explanations throughout about Japan's oldest beer (the brewery was founded in 1876). At the end there's a tasting salon (beers ¥200 to ¥300) where you can compare Sapporo's signature Black Label with Sapporo Classic (found only in Hokkaidō) and Kaitakushi Pilsner, a recreation of the original recipe (found only here).

Afterwards, head next door to the Sapporo Biergarten for more beer and jingisukan (all-you-can-eat lamb dish).

From the subway it's a 10-minute walk; the bus stops right out front.

Hokkaidō Museum

Museum in Sapporo

Details:

53-2 Konopporo, Atsubetsu-chō

Atsubetsu-ku

011-898-0466

http://www.hm.pref.hokkaido.lg.jp/

Hours: 9.30am-5pm May-Sep, to 4.30pm Oct-Apr

Price: adult/child/student ¥600/free/300

This recently renovated museum does an admirable job of explaining Hokkaidō's multilayered history, from the age of the woolly mammoths to the age of the steam locomotives, with English throughout. The museum is east of central Sapporo, in Nopporo Shinrin-kōen.

From Shin-Sapporo Station, take bus 新22 (¥210, 15 minutes, every 30 minutes) from bus stop 10 for Kaitaku-mura (開拓の村) and get off at the Hokkaidō hakubutsukan stop.

Parks in Sapporo

Ōdōri-kōen

Top choice park in Sapporo

Details:

http://www.sapporo-park.or.jp/odori/

This haven in the heart of the city is fully 13 blocks (1.5km) long, with the TV Tower at its eastern end. Among the green lawns and flower gardens are benches, fountains and sculptures; don't miss Noguchi Isamu's elegant Black Slide Mantra. This is also where many of the city's major events and festivals take place.

The park is a 10-minute walk south from JR Sapporo Station along Eki-mae-dōri.

Buildings, shrines and breweries in Sapporo

Kaitaku-mura

Historic Building in Sapporo

Details:

50-1 Konopporo, Atsubetsu-chō

Atsubetsu-ku

011-898-2692

http://www.kaitaku.or.jp/

Hours: 9am-5pm May-Sep, 9am-4.30pm Tue-Sun Oct-Apr

Price: adult/child/student ¥800/free/600

This expansive collection of historical buildings (and some recreations), in Nopporo Shinrin-kōen east of central Sapporo, shows the diversity of experience in 19th-century Hokkaidō. There are ornate, Victorian town halls; equally grand villas built by herring barons in the traditional Japanese style; and thatched-roof pioneer cabins. Most of the buildings you can enter.

From Shin-Sapporo Station, take bus 新22 (¥210, 15 minutes, every 30 minutes) from bus stop 10 for Kaitaku-mura (開拓の村), the last stop.

Centennial Memorial Tower

Monument in Sapporo

Details:

53-2 Konopporo, Atsubetsu-chō

Atsubetsu-ku

Construction of this modernist tower, designed by architect Iguchi Ken, started in 1968 to mark Sapporo's centennial (it was completed in 1970). The footprint is a hexagon, to evoke a six-sided snowflake; a cross-section reveals the kanji for 'north' (北; kita). It's in Nopporo Shinrin-kōen, a short walk behind the Hokkaidō Museum.

Old Hokkaidō Government Office Building

Notable Building in Sapporo

Details:

N3W6 Chūō-ku

011-204-5019

Hours: 8.45am-6pm

Known by all as Akarenga (red bricks), this magnificent neo-baroque building was constructed of bricks in 1888 and is surrounded by lovely lawns and gardens. There are various historical exhibits and shows from local artists inside. While Akarenga closes at 6pm, the gardens are open until 9pm and are a popular place for a stroll.

Hokkaidō Brewery

Brewery in Sapporo

Details:

542-1 Toiso

Eniwa

011-748-1876

http://www.sapporoholdings.jp/english/guide/hokkaido/

Hours: tours 10am-4pm Tue-Sun

This is one of the current brewing and bottling facilities for Sapporo beer. Guided tours are led (in Japanese only) by very enthusiastic brand ambassadors past windows that allow visitors to peer into the high-tech factory. You need to make reservations by 5pm the day before (best get a Japanese-speaker to do this). Note that the facility is not in operation every day; when you reserve be sure to ask. Either way, you get two free beers at the end!

Hokkaidō Brewery is a 40-minute train ride from Sapporo; take the JR Chitose line towards the airport and get off at JR Sapporo Beer Teien Station. There are a few luggage-sized lockers here if you're coming from/going to the airport.

Hokkaidō University

University in SapporoDetails

5N8W Kita-ku

http://www.hokudai.ac.jp/en/index.html

Hours: dawn-dusk

Established in 1876 this university is a scenic spot, with a number of unique buildings, including the Furukawa Memorial Hall and the Seikatei. The bust of William S Clark, the founding vice-president of the university, is a well-known landmark.

Tower Three-Eight

Observatory in Sapporo

Details:

JR Tower, JR Sapporo Station

011-209-5500

http://www.jr-tower.com/t38

Hours: 10am-11pm

Price: adult/child ¥720/300

Defeating Sapporo TV Tower when it comes to views and class (but not cultural significance!), the 38-floor JR Tower (173m) has a spacious observatory with seats and sofas. Best at night. Enter from the 6th floor of JR Tower East.

Sapporo Clock Tower

Historic Building in Sapporo

Details:

N1W2 Chūō-ku

http://sapporoshi-tokeidai.jp/

Hours: 8.45am-5pm

Price: adult/child ¥200/free

No Japanese tourist can leave Sapporo without snapping a photo of the city's signature landmark and oldest building, the clock tower. Built in 1878, the clock has not missed tolling the hour for more than 130 years. Inside is a museum on the tower.

Hokkaidō-jingū

Shinto Shrine in Sapporo

Details:

474 Miyagaoka Chūō-ku

http://www.hokkaidojingu.or.jp/eng/index.html

Dating back to 1869, this is one of the oldest shrines in Hokkaidō and is known for its spectacular cherry and plum blossoms in spring. It's inside sprawling, woodsy Maruyama-kōen (円山公園).

Hokkaidō road trip: exploring Japan's wild north

With its wide-open spaces, national parks, active volcanoes, forests of silvery beech, forlorn coastlines and remote fishing towns, Hokkaidō is ideal for road trips.

Japan is famous for its efficient rail system and doesn't exactly scream road trip. But when most people think of Japan, they usually don't think of Hokkaidō. In contrast to Japan's densely populated main island of Honshū, Hokkaidō is home to just 5% of Japan's population on 20% of its land. There are trains here too, of course, but the network is limited. Even Hokkaidō's cities, laid out in neat grids of wide streets, are easy to navigate by car.

Explore Japan's northernmost island with your own wheels and you'll have the freedom to detour to sapphire-blue caldera lakes, stop to dip in seaside hot springs, and pull over wherever fresh seafood beckons. Another bonus: accommodation and food are both cheaper on unfussy Hokkaidō than on Honshū.

Hakodate to Sapporo

Hakodate is Hokkaidō's southernmost port, where car ferries from Honshū disembark – and where you're now able to arrive via shinkansen (bullet train) from Tokyo and other points south through the Seikan Tunnel – making it a great road-trip starting point. Hakodate's two big attractions are its morning market and the night view from the top of Hakodate-yama. The market is a showcase for the rich bounty of Hokkaidō's seas, which you can sample in the form of kaisen-don, a dish of raw seafood on rice, at Kikuyo Shokudō (hakodate-kikuyo.com).

From Hakodate there are a couple of onsen (hot spring) options: the steaming hell pits of Hokkaidō's most famous onsen, Noboribetsu, or the casual seaside pools at Mizunashi Kaihin Onsen (or both). The latter is on the Kameda Peninsula east of Hakodate, and is regulated by the tides. Noboribetsu is north of the city, along the coastal highway heading towards Sapporo. You know you're getting close when you can smell the sulphur. Indeed, you can follow your nose to a number of onsen in Hokkaidō.

Continue on to Sapporo, the capital of Hokkaidō and the only place on the island that feels urban. The city is short on major sights but big on food and drink: it's the home of Sapporo beer and miso ramen. Outside the city, you can tour the Hokkaidō Brewery. You'll also be grateful for your wheels when you head out to Menya Saimi (5-3-12, 10-jō Misono, Toyohira-ku; 011-820-

6511), arguably Sapporo's best ramen shop, located in an otherwise nondescript residential neighborhood.

Both Hakodate and Sapporo have scores of good-value business hotels with double rooms for around ¥6000 (US$50). Noboribetsu is an onsen town with many places to stay, including sprawling Dai-ichi Takimoto-kan.

Sapporo to Daisetsuzan National Park & Akan National Park

You can think of Hokkaidō as having three distinct routes: the northern coast, the southern coast and the dead center. The central route towards Akan National Park is far and away the most interesting, passing Daisetsuzan National Park. This is Hokkaidō's largest park, with several volcanic mountain ranges, alpine meadows and a good deal of wildlife. You can base yourself for a couple of days at one of the three onsen towns, Asahidake, Sōunkyō and Tokachi-dake, and hit the trails. Count yourself lucky if you can secure one of the six rooms at Lodge Nutapukaushipe, an eccentric log house with wood-burning stoves. En route to Daisetsuzan, it's worth taking a detour to Biei, where a network of country lanes winds through fields of wildflowers.

The other attractive option from Sapporo – especially for those with a fondness for stretches of desolate coastline – is to take the long northern route up to Wakkanai, a very windy former trading post from where ferries depart to remote Rebun-tō and Rishiri-tō. From Wakkanai, you can continue down Rte 238 along the Sea of Okhotsk. (You could also do this stretch on the way to Akan and visit Daisetsuzan on the way back to Sapporo.)

Whichever path you take, you'll want to see Akan National Park, home to several brilliantly blue caldera lakes. From the Bihoro Pass there's a spectacular view of Kussharo-ko, Japan's largest caldera lake, and its central island Naka-jima. There's also a somewhat touristy Ainu Village on the shores of Akan-ko and a fantastic lodge near Kussharo-ko, Marukibune, serving traditional Ainu dishes.

Akan to Rausu & Nemuro

From Akan National Park head north until you reach Rte 334 on the coast, then turn east towards the Shiretoko Peninsula. At the end of the road is the waterfall, Kamuiwakka-yu-no-taki. You can take a dip (in a swimsuit) in the fall's lower pool; the water is warm as the river above is fed from a hot spring. Beyond is Shiretoko National Park – true wilderness, as no cars are allowed in. If you want to pause your road trip, consider tackling the Shiretoko Traverse, a two-day hike that spans the park. Otherwise you can enjoy the scenery while driving through the Shiretoko Pass, which goes by mountain Rausu-dake and beech forests. On the other side of the peninsula, on the Nemuro Strait, Rte 87 runs up the coast nearly to the tip. Here there are a couple of teeny-tiny onsen, such as Seseki Onsen. In the evening, the harbors on the east coast are illuminated by the lights of squid boats night fishing.

Nemuro is the other little finger stretching out on Hokkaidō's east coast. At the tip, Nosappu-misaki marks the easternmost part of Japan – those islands you can see on the horizon are Russia. There's not much else to see here, but there is a good place to eat: Suzuki Shokudō (32 Nosappu, Nemuro; 0153-28-3198) draws visitors from afar for its sanma-don (raw Pacific saury on rice) and its signature way of doing miso soup with a whole crab in it. The diner also runs a small raidā hausu (rider house), dirt-cheap dorm-style accommodation for motorcyclists and cyclists, of which Hokkaidō has many.

From Nemuro you can take Rte 44 down to Kushiro to visit the Japanese Crane Reserve. Kushiro also has an airport with flights back to Tokyo. Or continue down to Tomakomai, where you can catch the car ferry (sunflower.co.jp) that runs all the way to Oarai in Ibaraki (two hours north of Tokyo) in 17.5 hours. There is a public bath and a movie theatre on board!

Road-trip tips

The best time of year to drive around Hokkaidō is mid-May through mid-October. Any later and snow threatens to cover mountain passes and ice can be a problem. Note that Daisetsuzan is the first place in Japan to see snow, usually in September. You might also want to give crowded July and August a miss.

For a route heading from Hakodate to Kushiro, budget at least a week to allow for sightseeing, soaking and hiking time. In 10 days you could also go up to Wakkanai and visit the islands Rebun-tō and Rishiri-tō. But to get the most out of your time, take the one-way trip through the central Hokkaidō, return the car at the other end and fly out.

Nippon Rent-a-Car Hokkaidō (nrh.co.jp) has offices at all airports in Hokkaidō and major train stations, such as Hakodate, Sapporo and Abashiri. It is possible to pick up and drop off the car at different locations. Some cars are equipped with English GPS systems.

Navigating in Japan is easier than you might think: rental cars come standard with GPS devices that allow you to program the phone number of your destination (much easier than imputing complicated Japanese addresses).

Hokkaidō's roads are well paved and well signposted in English. What you won't see noted in English is road closures, so if you're travelling around the shoulder periods (April, May, October and November), it's a good idea to run your route by someone before heading out. You'll also need to keep an eye on the speedometer (as the limits can be irrationally low) and look out for wildlife, such as deer.

Most towns will have a petrol station and a convenience store, though it is wise to not let yourself get under half a tank. Many petrol stations close around 7pm or 8pm.

Hokkaidō has dozens of campgrounds – you can search the full list at the official tourism website (en.visit-hokkaido2.jp). Those on two wheels can also take advantage of the region's network of rider houses, listed at Hatinosu (hatinosu.net, in Japanese); these can fill up fast in the summer so it's smart to ring ahead.

For more information on driving in Hokkaidō, see the tourism bureau's downloadable handbook (hkd.mlit.go.jp), in English.

Kobe

Perched on a hillside sloping down to the sea, Kōbe (神戸) is one of Japan's most attractive and cosmopolitan cities. It was a maritime gateway from the earliest days of trade with China and home to one of the first foreign communities after Japan reopened to the world in the mid-19th century.

Kōbe's relatively small size makes it a pleasure for casual wandering and stopping in its high-quality restaurants and cafes. The most pleasant neighborhoods to explore are Kitano-chō, Nankinmachi Chinatown and, after dark, the bustling nightlife districts around Sannomiya Station.

Kōbe's two main gateways are Sannomiya and Shin-Kōbe stations, with easy access to sights, lodging and dining on foot or a short train ride away. Shinkansen trains stop at Shin-Kōbe Station, uphill in the northeast corner of the city center – a quick subway ride or 20-minute walk connects the two stations.

Shinto shrines in Kobe

Ikuta Shrine

Shinto Shrine in Kōbe

Details:

1-2-1 Shimo-Yamate-dōri

078-321-3851

Hours: 7am-sunset

Said to date from AD 201, this peaceful, wooden shrine has played a key role in sake-brewing history; it has survived civil wars (notably as a hideout for the Heike clan) and WWII, and been a gathering place for residents after natural disasters such as the 1995 earthquake. Plaques in front of the main building commemorate generations of emperors' visits, and around the back a forest and landmark camphor tree provide a break from the city's bustle.

Kitano Tenman-jinja

Shinto Shrine in Kōbe

Details:

3-12-1 Kitano-chō, Chūō-ku

078-221-2139

Hours: 7am-5pm

This lovely little shrine to academic pursuits holds pride of place in Kitano-chō, up a steep hill and past a touristy stretch of souvenir and snack shops. Even if you aren't studying for an upcoming exam, it's a great place to take a breather, do some lazy people-watching and gaze all the way across town to the Inland Sea.

Museums in Kobe

Hakutsuru Sake Brewery Museum

Brewery in Kōbe

Details:

4-5-5 Sumiyoshi Minami-machi, Higashinada-ku

078-822-8907

http://www.hakutsuru-sake.com/

Hours: 9.30am-4.30pm

Hakutsuru is the dominant sake brewer in Kōbe's Nada-gogō district, one of Japan's major sake-brewing centers. The self-guided tour through its historic, wooden former brewery building (the current, giant brewery is behind it) is a fascinating look into traditional sake-making methods; life-sized models appear on old equipment, and a pamphlet and videos in English help explain. A free sake tasting is available after the tour.

Take the Hanshin line eight stops east from Sannomiya to Sumiyoshi Station (¥190, seven minutes if you switch trains at Mikage, 15 minutes if you take the futsū (local) train; express trains do not stop). Exit the station, walk south to the elevated highway and cross the pedestrian overpass, make a U-turn at the bottom of the steps, take your first left, then a right; the entrance is on the right. Use the blue-and-white crane logo atop the factory as your guide.

Other destinations in Kobe

Nunobiki Falls

Waterfall in Kōbe

You'd never guess that such a beautiful natural sanctuary could sit so close to the city. This revered waterfall in four sections (the longest is 43m tall) has been the subject of art, poetry and worship for centuries – some of the poems are reproduced on stone tablets at the site. It's accessible by a steep 400m path, from Shin-Kōbe Station. Take the ground-floor exit, turn left and walk under the station building to the path.

Note: the hike up the stone steps can leave you a sweaty mess, especially in summer – take it nice and slow and enjoy the river views as you ascend. Alternatively, access the falls in about 30 downhill minutes from the lower exit of Nunobiki Herb Gardens, by the midway station of the ropeway (go past the reservoir). One-way fare on the ropeway is ¥700 in either direction between the midway and lower stations.

Port of Kōbe Earthquake Memorial Park

Monument in Kōbe

Details:

Meriken Park

At 5.46am on 17 January 1995 the Great Hanshin Earthquake struck this region. It was Japan's strongest since the Great Kantō Quake of 1923 devastated Tokyo. Kōbe bore the brunt of the damage – 6000 killed, 40,000-plus casualties, toppled expressways and nearly 300,000 lost buildings. This simple, open-air, harbor side museum tells the story in artefacts and a video presentation in English. Most striking is a section of the dock that was left as it was after that devastating day.

The Memorial Park is in Meriken Park, a short walk from the Maritime Museum & Kawasaki Good Times World.

Notable areas in Kobe

Kitano-chō

Area in Kōbe

Details:

Hours: most ijinkan open 9am-6pm, to 5pm Oct-Mar

Price: ijinkan ¥350-750, combination tickets ¥1300-3000

For generations of Japanese tourists, this pleasant, hilly neighborhood is Kōbe, thanks to the dozen or so well-preserved homes of (mostly) Western trading families and diplomats who settled here during the Meiji period. Its winding streets, nostalgic brick- and weatherboard-built ijinkan (literally 'foreigners' houses'), cafes, restaurants and, yes, souvenir shops are great for exploring. All lend a European-American atmosphere, though admittedly it's probably less intriguing for Western visitors than for Japanese.

Not sure you want to invest the time or effort? Stop for a coffee at the Starbucks concept store in a former ijinkan c 1907. If you like it, continue uphill to the rest of the ijinkan.

Nankinmachi

Area in Kōbe

Four traditional gates mark the entrances to this gaudy, bustling, unabashedly touristy collection of Chinese restaurants and trinket and medicinal herb stores. The offerings should be familiar to anyone who's visited Chinatowns elsewhere, it's fun for a stroll, particularly at night when lights illuminate elaborately painted shop facades. Restaurants tend toward the overPriced and may disappoint sophisticated palates (set meals from about ¥850), although it's one of the few places in Japan where street snacking is condoned (snacks from about ¥200).

Notable buildings and sights in Kobe

Akashi Kaikyō Bridge

Bridge in Kōbe

Details:

2051 Higashi-Maikō-chō

Tarumi-ku

078-784-3339

Hours: promenade 9am-6pm, exhibition center 9.15am-5pm Mar–mid-Jul & Sep-Nov, to 6pm mid-Jul–Aug, to 4.30pm Dec-Feb

Price: ¥310

West of central Kōbe is Japan's tallest bridge (283m), across the Akashi Strait. See it up close at the Maikō Marine Promenade, a 320m walkway 47m above sea level, over the bridge's northern end – try not to freak out over the glass floors! An indoor lounge features a 360-degree camera from atop a stanchion. Nearby, Akashi Kaikyō Bridge Exhibition Centre explains the science behind bridge building, through videos in English and exhibits including a cross-section of the 1.1m-diameter main cable.

City Hall Observation Lobby

Viewpoint in Kōbe

Details:

6-5-1 Kanō-chō, Chūō-ku

078-331-8181

Hours: 8.15am-10pm Mon-Fri, 10am-10pm Sat & Sun

Get a bird's eye orientation to the city – and appreciate its breadth – from the 24th floor of Kōbe City Hall. It's particularly romantic and impressive around sunset as the sky changes colors and the city lights up at your feet. During the day, weather permitting, you can see all the way to Kansai International Airport across Osaka Bay.

There are also display cases saluting Kōbe's sister cities, plus a cafe and Korean restaurant.

Kōbe Nunobiki Herb Gardens & Ropeway

Gardens in Kōbe

Details:

Hours: herb gardens 10am-5pm, ropeway 9.30am-4.45pm, longer hours summer & weekends Sep-Nov

Price: ropeway one-way/return incl. herb gardens admission ¥900/1400 (¥800 return after 5pm), herb garden admission only ¥200

Escape the city on a 400m-high mountain ridge, with sweeping views across town to the bay. Access is via ropeway (cable car) departing from near Shin-Kōbe Station. Some twee shops and restaurants near the top station mark the entrance to the Herb Gardens, which has 14 themed areas from Japanese to English, connected by paved path downhill to the ropeway's mid-station for your ride back down. Alternatively, the path continues down to Nunobiki Falls, about 30 minutes, and Shin-Kōbe Station.

Mt Fuji

Of all Japan's iconic images, Mt Fuji (富士山; 3776m) is the real deal. Admiration for the mountain appears in Japan's earliest recorded literature, dating from the 8th century. Back then the now dormant volcano was prone to spewing smoke, making it all the more revered. In 2013, the year Fuji-san was granted World Heritage status, some 300,000 people climbed the country's highest peak.

The Japanese proverb 'He who climbs Mt Fuji once is a wise man, he who climbs it twice is a fool' remains as valid as ever. While reaching the top brings a great sense of achievement (particularly at sunrise), be aware that it's a grueling climb not known for its beautiful scenery or for being at one with nature. During the climbing season routes are packed, and its barren apocalyptic-looking landscape is a world away from Fuji's beauty when viewed from afar. At the summit, the crater has a circumference of 4km, but be prepared for it to be clouded over.

Activities in Mt Fuji

Climbing Mt Fuji: Know Before You Go

Make no mistake: Mt Fuji is a serious mountain, high enough for altitude sickness, and on the summit it can go from sunny and warm to wet, windy and cold remarkably quickly. Even if conditions are fine, you can count on it being close to freezing in the morning, even in summer. Also be aware that visibility can rapidly disappear with a blanket of mist rolling in suddenly.

At a minimum, bring clothing appropriate for cold and wet weather, including a hat and gloves. Also bring at least two liters of water (you can buy more on the mountain during the climbing season), as well as a map and snacks. If you're climbing at night, bring a torch (flashlight) or headlamp, and spare batteries. Also bring plenty of cash for buying snacks, other necessities and souvenirs from the mountain huts and to use their toilets (¥200).

Descending the mountain is much harder on the knees than ascending; hiking poles will help. To avoid altitude sickness, be sure to take it slowly and take regular breaks. If you're suffering severe symptoms, you'll need to make an immediate descent.

For summit weather conditions, see www.snow-forecast.com/resorts/Mount-Fuji/6day/top.

Trails

The mountain is divided into 10 'stations' from base (First Station) to summit (Tenth). From the base station is the original pilgrim trail, but these days most climbers start from the halfway point at one of the four Fifth Stations, all of which can be accessed via bus or car. The intersection of trails is not well marked and it's easy to get lost, particularly on the way down, ending up at the wrong exit point; this is a good reason to climb with experienced guides.

To time your arrival for dawn you can either start up in the afternoon, stay overnight in a mountain hut and continue early in the morning, or climb the whole way at night. You do not want to arrive on the top too long before dawn, as it will be very cold and windy, even at the height of summer.

Fifth Station Routes

Around 90% of climbers opt for these more convenient, faster routes. The four routes are Yoshida Trail (2305m); Subashiri (1980m); Fujinomiya (2380m); and Gotemba (1440m). Allow five to six hours to reach the top (though some climb it in half the time) and about three hours to descend, plus 1½ hours for circling the crater at the top.

The Yoshida Trail is by far and away the most popular route. It's accessed from Fuji Subaru Line Fifth Station (aka Kawaguchi-ko Fifth Station), and has the most modern facilities and is easiest to reach from Kawaguchi-ko town.

The less trodden, but more scenic, forested Subashiri Trail is a good alternative. As it merges with the Yoshida Trail at the Eighth Station, it's possible to combine the two by heading up via the Yoshida path and descending via Subashiri by schussing down its loose volcanic sand. Though be aware you'll end up at Subashiri Fifth Station, so it might not be an option if you've parked your car at Kawaguchi-ko Fifth Station.

Other Fifth Stations are Fujinomiya, which is best for climbers coming from the west (Nagoya, Kyoto and beyond) and the seldom-used and neglected Gotemba Trail, a tough 7½-hour climb to the summit.

Traditional Route

Historically, Fuji pilgrims began at Sengen-jinja near present-day Fuji-Yoshida, paying their homage to the shrine gods before beginning their 19km ascent up the sacred mountain. Today the Yoshidaguchi Trail offers climbers a chance to participate in this centuries-old tradition. Purists will tell you this is the only way to climb, saying that the lower reaches are the most beautiful, through lush forests along an isolated path.

It takes about five hours to reach the old Yoshidaguchi Fifth Station – you can cut this down by half by catching the climbing-season bus from Fujisan Station to Umagaeshi (¥500).

The trail meets up with the one leaving from the Fuji Subaru Line Fifth Station (also known as Kawaguchi-ko Fifth Station) at the Sixth Station. Count on around 12 hours to complete the climb from Fuji's base to summit.

Fuji Subaru Line Fifth Station

he road to the Fifth Station from Kawaguchi-ko, on the Fuji Subaru Line, stays open as long as the weather permits (from roughly mid-April to early December). Even when summiting is off-limits, it's still possible to take the bus here just to stand in awesome proximity to the snowcapped peak.

From roughly mid-May to late October, you can hike the flat Ochūdō (御中道) trail that hugs the mountain at the tree line; it stretches 4km to Okuniwa (奥庭), where you'll have to double back. At either end of the climbing season, check conditions before setting out.

Sleeping

Conditions in mountain huts are Spartan (a blanket on the floor sandwiched between other climbers), but reservations are recommended and are essential on weekends. It's also important to let huts know if you decide to cancel at the last minute; be prepared to pay to cover the cost of your no show.

Camping on the mountain is not permitted, other than at the designated campsite near the Fuji Subaru Line Fifth Station (aka Kawaguchi-ko Fifth Station).

Eating

From the Fifth Stations up, dozens of mountain huts offer hikers simple hot meals in addition to a place to sleep. Most huts allow you to rest inside as long as you order something.

Resources

Climbing Mt Fuji (www17.plala.or.jp/climb_fujiyama) and the Official Web Site for Mt Fuji Climbing (www.fujisan-climb.jp) are good online resources. The Climbing Mt Fuji brochure, available at the Fuji-Yoshida or Kawaguchi-ko Tourist Information Centers, is also worth picking up.

Getting There & Away

For those wanting to start trekking as soon as they arrive from Tokyo, Keiō Dentetsu Bus runs direct buses (¥2700, 2½ hours; reservations necessary) from the Shinjuku Highway Bus Terminal to Fuji Subaru Line Fifth Station (aka Kawaguchi-ko Fifth Station; it does not operate in winter).

Buses run from both Kawaguchi-ko Station and Fujisan Station to the starting point at Fuji Subaru Line Fifth Station (one way/return ¥1540/2100, one hour) roughly mid-April to early December. In the trekking season, buses depart hourly from around 6.30am until 7pm (ideal for climbers intending to make an overnight ascent). Returning from Fifth Station, buses head back to town from 8am to 8.30pm.

In the off-season, the first bus inconveniently leaves Kawaguchi-ko and Fujisan Stations at 8.40am, and the last bus returns at 6.15pm, meaning most trekkers will need to get a taxi in the morning to have enough time (around ¥12,000, plus ¥2100 in tolls), before getting the bus back. The bus schedule is highly seasonal; call Fujikyū Yamanashi bus or your hotel for Details:.

In the low season you should be able to find other trekkers to share a taxi at K's House. Car hire is another option (particularly good if you're in a group), costing around ¥6800 per day plus fuel and tolls.

To get to the Subashiri Fifth Station trail, you can catch a bus from Kawaguchi-ko to Gotemba (¥1510), from where regular buses head to the Subashiri access point; Gotemba can also be accessed directly from Tokyo either by bus or train.

Internet Access

Free Wi-Fi is now available at Fifth Station access points and the summit, for 72 hours after you've acquired an access card at one of the Fifth Station information centers.

Conclusion

Thank you for purchasing and reading the Japan Travel Guide. I sincerely hope you have/have had a great time in Japan – it is a truly magical country. If you need more travel guides you can find them on my Amazon Author Page - https://www.amazon.com/Alec-Nowell/e/B0797RQSMJ.